Contents

Baa Baa Pink Sheep

A Devil's Dictionary for Modern Ireland

TERRY PRONE

LONDUBH

First published in 2015

Londubh Books
18 Casimir Avenue, Harold's Cross, Dublin 6w, Ireland
www.londubh.ie

1 3 5 4 2

Origination by Londubh Books; cover by Bluett
Printed by ScandBook AB, Falun, Sweden
ISBN: 978-1-907535-78-9

A Note on the Text
The text is set in Adobe Garamond Pro.
Headings are set in Goudy Old Style.

Acknowledgements

This book represents relentless exploitation of co-workers, friends and clients. Anton Savage, Eoghan McDermott and Lorcan Nyhan from the Training Clinic at The Communications Clinic provided some of the cleverer definitions but Barry McLaughlin brought an aggressively beyond-the-Pale viewpoint. Aileen Gaskin, Pauline Ní Luanaigh, Gearóid Rennicks and Olive Stephens in our Public Relations Clinic were generous with their time and wildly varying lexicons.

Writer Miriam O'Callaghan, once the book was mentioned to her, produced so many words and definitions so quickly, we figure she missed several deadlines in the process.

Stefanie Preissner, encountered just as the book went to press, volunteered a rake of misused words and definitions. None of them in rhyme.

Stephanie Brady organised everything. But then, she always does.

The wonderful Ronan Casey, star of print, radio and music, provided the titles. Meaning the one I wanted (*Baa, Baa, Bullshit*) and the one I was allowed to have. His latest book, *Medium-Sized Town, Fairly Big Story* figures in the Bibliography. As well as in all good bookshops.

Introduction

He had stripey knickers and wasn't animated, so it was a miracle that Dáithí Lacha was ever made into a TV series, but it was one, in the 1960s. The commentary was in Irish, so a generation of kids was forced to watch the frame-by-frame non-event that was David Duck's life. *Dáithí Lacha* made *Bosco* look as subtle as a Chekov play. The man behind it, Flann O'Riain, also drew newspaper cartoons under the name DOLL and he maintained that whenever he ran out of ideas, he would pick up his paperback copy of *The Devil's Dictionary* because, by opening it at random, he would encounter a word definition so skewed or amusing it would jolt him out of cartoonist's block. He evangelised on behalf of the book, persuading me, when I interviewed him for a radio programme, to invest in a copy. I still have it.

The original *Devil's Dictionary* started in 1881 as an occasional satirical newspaper series written by Ambrose Bierce, a soldier and writer born in Ohio. Known as Bitter Bierce because of the venom of his literary criticism, Bierce set off for Mexico in 1913 to cover the war there and evaporated. Nobody knows what happened to him. He left behind him fine reportage of the wars in which he had fought and a considerable body of fiction which led to his attaining the reputation of finest short story writer of the 19th century.

The *Dictionary* has been in print for more than a century, despite doing an initial sales faceplant because the publishers, who were a small bit religious, felt they'd be singled out for a thunderbolt if they put Satan in the title. Instead, it came out as *The Cynic's Word Book*, which did it no favours, because it joined a bunch of books with 'Cynic' in the title, none of which was any good. It will be understood that this did nothing to sweeten up Bitter Bierce.

Some of Bierce's definitions, read in the 21st century, are squirmingly embarrassing. What was correct back then has not always sustained its correctness. Some of them, however, have taken on a life of their own and are often assumed to be the work of that other great quote-meister, Mark Twain. A bride, for example, Bierce defined as 'A woman with a fine prospect of happiness behind her.' Similarly, his definition of a bore is relatively mild: 'A person who talks when you wish him to listen.'

Bierce included quotations from great writers and parodies of their work and veered from extreme brevity to extreme length in the definitions. His negative cast of mind led to defining a politician as 'An eel in the fundamental mud upon which the superstructure of organized society is reared. When he wriggles he mistakes the agitation of his tail for the trembling of the edifice. As compared with the statesman, he suffers the disadvantage of being alive.'

Since Bierce's time, the lexicon has been so enriched by time and Irishness that an Irish version seemed overdue.

A-list: In the past, used to separate those famous for doing something superbly from the rest. Now mainly used as hopeless-case seduction, as in 'How to get an A-list body before your holidays.'

Absolutely: How guests on radio programmes answer questions from lousy interviewers who incorporate every bit of inform-ation on the topic into a lengthy statement they then dress up as a question by putting an upward inflection at the end of it.

Across it: Spreads a human being's responsibility like a thrown tarpaulin: 'Pádraig is across that.' Meaning 'Pádraig has been put in charge of that' or 'given responsibility for that'.

Acronym: Also known as an initialism, it is a word made up of the first letter of each word in a longer phrase. So Acquired Immune Deficiency Syndrome became AIDS, knocking hell out of any prospect of an eponymous brand of slimming biscuits recovering from its decline. Initialisms came into common use in the Second World War, with divisions of the US navy and air force adopting them. Then came a wave of phrases condensed into their capital letters, including: ASAP: as soon as possible; BTW: by the way; FWIW: for what it's worth; LGTB: lesbian, gay, transgender and bisexual; FYI: for your information; IMHO: in my humble opinion; and TBJ: thanks be to Jasus.

Increasingly, brands are going the acronym route. Think HSE, RSA, HIQA and a myriad others. Some, like KFC, went that way because the word 'fried' became associated with obesity and they believed – probably correctly – that this would be lost in the letters. Without acronyms texts, whatsapps and tweets would be lost for words, because TBLR (they breed like rabbits).

Ad blocking software: The best thing since the sliced pan. Maybe even better. Allows use of websites without being beaten over the head or generally harassed from all sides by advertising. Go monetise somewhere else, lads.

ADHD: One of the most popular diagnoses in paediatric medicine in the western world. Parents who have a child who won't sit still in school, doesn't pay attention to details, is easily distracted and talks the legs off the teacher are likely to be advised either that their offspring is 'gifted' or might have ADHD. Understandably, if their child seems wired to the moon, they grab at the possibility of a diagnosis and the chance to have the kid suppressed by medication. Not that any parent of a child so diagnosed ever thinks of themselves as suppressing their son or daughter by medication.

Back in 1937, a Dr Charles Bradley noticed that some frenetic children had a paradoxical response to stimulant medication. In other words, pills that allowed adults to stay awake way past their bedtime had the opposite effect on excitable children. They calmed them down. From then on, the manufacturers of Ritalin and related medications were on a roll (their popularity increased in recent times when they began to be used as adult slimming aids and as a way of helping older students concentrate during exams).

'The symptoms of distractability and impulsivity are all too real but we're using an outdated, invalid definition of ADHD, one that has been kept in place for decades by physicians and other practitioners, pharmaceutical companies, the media and even patients themselves,' says Professor Richard Saul, who maintains, not that ADHD is over-diagnosed but that it doesn't exist at all. 'The millions of false diagnoses result in a cascade of consequences including delayed or denied treatment, spiraling health-care costs and significant health risks and frustration for patients and their families.'*

Adolescence: Eight years in a young person's life that age their parents – on average – by twenty. Adolescence is hormones on the hoof, rebellion rampant, leaving no door unslammed. It's when they take your lovely kid away and replace him or her with a vile simulacrum who hates and despises you. The good news is they give your real kid back at around age nineteen. Mark Twain's experience gives the other side of this story: 'When I was fourteen, I thought my father was so stupid I could hardly stand to have the old man around. But when I got to twenty-one, I was astonished by how much he had learned in seven years.'

Affirmation: New age prayers, uttered morning and night to convince the utterers that they're doing better than they really are. Émile Coué, a French apothecary who died in 1926, was a big believer in affirmations, urging followers to repeat, immeasurable times, 'Every day in every way, I'm getting better and better.' Which kind of covers all the self-delusion options, the way we see it. It's now possible to get an app, for free, which will give you a fresh affirmation every day to improve your life.

After: Word used, in mainstream and social media, to make nonsense of the story it graces. 'Man killed after car collides with

---

* Richard Saul, M.D., *ADHD Does Not Exist: The Truth about Attention Deficit and Hyperactivity Disorder*, New York: Harper Wave, 2014.

truck.' Poor guy. First his car T-bones a truck and then someone comes along and kills him just for spite.

Age: Research has shown that the younger your personally-perceived age, the longer you are going to live. This emerged in *JAMA* (*Journal of Internal Medicine*), where researchers Isla Rippon and Andrew Steptoe published a study of the link between mortality and perceived age rather than years. People in the first group felt themselves to be older than their chronological age. The individuals in a second group perceived themselves as younger than their actual age. Those in the third group boringly felt themselves to be roughly their actual age. For no obvious reason, the researchers, when they tracked the participants over a few years, established that the folk who thought they were younger than they really were were significantly less likely to die from a range of killer diseases. In other words, if you accept chronology or if you see yourself as older than you really are, the bad news is that you are likely to pop your clogs sooner than the mad yokes who live in denial.

Ageism: Fear of being accused of ageism is why the Beeb employs Mary Berry and Prue Leith. According to Prue Leith.

Ageless: What any celeb over eighty is described as being.

Agenda: A contents list dreamed up five minutes before a meeting, designed to persuade all participants that, at the end of an essentially random chat, they will have achieved something by covering all the items listed. This is never the case but has led to a widespread myth that once you have an agenda, you will have a good meeting. This is roughly the same as believing that once you have a dead cow, you will have a good dinner.

Agricultural: Used in the pejorative sense to indicate a lack of finesse or grace. Leinster rugby fans describe Munster rugby as 'agricultural' when they have been beaten for the umpteenth time in Thomond Park. Also used to describe diesel engines in vehicles that cost less than €15,000 new.

Ah, here: A uniquely Irish response to an unexpected demand or annoyance. Incorporates 'Give me a break', 'Puhlease' and 'For the love of Jasus.'

Alcohol: The liquid end result of letting things go off and then boiling them. Creates a transient high accompanied by inability to make sense and loss of balance, followed by vomiting, dehydration, missing work and massive depression. Cheap. Handy. (Turn left after the frozen foods in your local supermarket.) The single biggest source of collective delusion, led by those who believe themselves to be moderate drinkers and who maintain that a glass of wine at the end of the day is necessary to sustain the stress of being a mum. The wine glass used is the size of a water-cooler bottle. This glass of wine each weekday night, combined with a bottle each night at the weekend, has changed cirrhosis of the liver from a disease of old men into one of young women.

Allergy: Tell anyone who has had anaphylactic shock that you are 'allergic' to wheat because it makes you bloat and it is likely they will slit your throat. Rightly so. True allergy can kill.

Alickadoo: A term, insulting in intent, for administrative members of rugby clubs – the ones who wear blazers and control tickets. Inapplicable to GAA, which has its own forms of denigration.

All to play for: A general election cliché used by commentators who haven't a clue and lack the courage to admit it.

Alpha: The first letter in the Greek alphabet, which has been lifted and applied elsewhere to denote the first or most notable or most powerful element in any mix. Hence, the alpha dog is the leader of the pack. The alpha male ditto. Recently applied even more promiscuously to fashion: the alpha bag, the alpha shoes and the alpha jacket.

Already: I'm bored already. So stop it already. What is this rubbish? Already?

Alzheimers: The decline into dementia taken by some close relatives as giving permission to share with the world details of the life of the demented person, particularly those recording the diminution of their competence, in a way which would have horrified the betrayed individuals. Most notable in this respect was Iris Murdoch's husband, John Bayley, an Oxford don who held back not a whit when producing *Elegy for Iris* (1999), which turned him into an international literary figure and ensured (according to himself) that when Iris died, he was besieged by people, including women eager to share the elderly man's bed. The nakedly revealing *Elegy* may have been good for Bayley, who, basking in the late fame generated by the book and subsequent film, gave countless interviews about marrying again a year after Murdoch died but it was certainly not good for the memory of Iris Murdoch, whose privacy was grievously invaded when no right of reply existed for her.

Amazing: Mildly pleasing.

Amazon: In the last great wave of industrial development, manufacturers like Guinness and Cadburys went out of their way to take care of their employees. Workers were proud – and relieved – to say they worked for Guinness, which had inarguably the best welfare and sickness support systems at the time. Cadburys actually built a town called Bournville to move their workers out of smog-polluted central Birmingham. They surrounded the factory with newly-built homes, schools, civic buildings and churches. It was part of the Quaker ethos. On the other hand, the Jeff Bezos ethos, over at Amazon, has been called 'a purposeful form of Darwinism'. In other words, if you survive, this, in and of itself, makes you fit to hand on your genes to the next generation of Amazon wage slaves.

Ambitious: A swear word when applied to women.

An Taisce: Voluntary organisation devoted to muttering: 'Down with that sort of thing' at everything new in the built environment. Nine times out of ten, they're right. Nine times out of ten, you wish they weren't.

Anchor baby: Derogatory term applied to the offspring of illegal immigrants in the United States, describing any offspring of a couple born in America, which makes the child an American citizen and makes the deportation of their parents much more difficult. Public use of the term in August 2015 did Jeb Bush's presidential hopes no good at all.

And that was just: Form of humour where a particular set of behaviours are listed for the reader to assume that they apply to the main characters in the narrative, only to have the rug pulled from under that assumption. *The Irish Times* sportswriter, Keith Duggan, describing the 2015 Mayo-Dublin semi-final, used the device thus: 'Supporters in the upper house of Croke Park looked down to see men felled with cramp and fatigue, gasping for oxygen and water. And that was just in the ard-chomhairle [GAA central council]. What was happening out on the football field was on an entirely different plane.'

Angels: Mythical winged creatures who have a lot more to be doing with their time than hanging around people's hair, as claimed by a bestselling book on the topic, or investing themselves in toys, cards or brooches carrying boundless significance for the determinedly trivial.

Anger: Euphemism for permanent bad temper.

Angle grinder: An implement for cutting steel, casual mention of which gives a man a deep conviction of his own virility.

Anthem: Theme song of the nation, the UK's currently being 'God Save the Queen'. Jeremy Corbyn distinguished himself in his first week as leader of the Labour Party by standing, mute, in a much-photographed line-up of other eminences, each of whom gave it socks. He gave it silence. The *Telegraph*, for once, was not on its own in jumping up and down on a left-winger. He then said he'd sing it in future, which must be such a consolation to her record-breaking Majesty.

Anxiety: The intelligent response to being broke, breaking up with a partner, or being canned from your job. Now subject to the administration of medication.

Apocrypha: Stuff nobody may ever have said but that lots of people would like to believe someone did say. Classic example: 'Mandelson asked me for 10 pence to ring a friend. I said 'Here's 20 pence. Ring them all.'

Appearance: Largely irrelevant for men, although baldness is pejoratively commented upon. *The Financial Times* columnist Lucy Kellaway, when she attended a gathering of the four big accountancy firms in Britain, noticed that, out of the eighty faces present, male and female, none was ugly: 'Not only have we banished the ugly from most competitive jobs,' she says, 'polite society has banished the word, too. In time, the U-word will be deemed as obnoxious as the N-word but for now I'm using it to make a point.

No one calls anyone ugly. They just decline to hire them. We aren't sexist or racist any more but are still hopelessly faceist…recruiters and managers are so faceist that the good-looking have been found to earn some 10 per cent more than the bad-looking; while the chief executives with commanding faces have been shown to run companies that make the fattest profits.'

Appearance, for women, is now more important than it ever was, which goes to prove that the feminism of the last century face-planted, big-time, on this issue.

The 1970s feminists believed they could get models removed from the bonnets of cars in advertisements (fail) render fatness or plainness irrelevant in career terms (fail) and prevent the judgement of any woman starting with the size of her boobs (mega fail).

Female politicians are particularly afflicted by the appearance issue. Good-looking candidates or TDs/senators have a massive brand advantage, not least because they appear in photographs hundreds of times more often than their less attractive sisters. Women politicians who don't reach the implicit standard are subjected to hostile comment and coverage.

Former Australian Prime Minister Julia Gillard said that while individual examples seem trivial, the totality of the way media treated her during her three years at the top of Oz politics demonstrated the difference between how male and female politicians are filmed.

'There's the television footage taken from behind of me getting into a car, the lens trained on my bottom, not something done to male prime ministers,' she says. 'Even before Germaine Greer's attention-seeking outburst about my body shape and clothing, apparently my arse was newsworthy. The front-page image, followed by a full-page frame-by-frame spread of me tripping over in India. No prime ministerial stumble, even John Howard's physical stumble at a time he was politically stumbling, warranted a frame-by-frame front-page spread in the *Daily Telegraph*. Howard's stumble was reported on page 5. A television network commissioning and airing a full comedy series about my prime ministership. Something never done before and with no signs of it being done again now we have a male prime minister.'

The Germaine Greer 'outburst' mentioned, by the way, saw the Australian author and academic, who has always maintained that women shouldn't be judged by their physical attributes, describe the then prime minister as having 'a big arse' in a rant about what was wrong with her jackets. While not repeating the 'big arse' phrase, Greer went on, in other appearances, to recommend that Gillard get a good dressmaker. She hasn't, to our knowledge, reflected on the arse size or tailoring of any prominent male politician. Ah, sisterhood...

Apolitical: Verbal method of disengagement from door-to-door political canvassers as they hand out their leaflets: 'Thank you but I am apolitical.' Fianna Fáil maintain the phrase is a dead giveaway that the user supports Fine Gael.

Apology: A lost art.

Has morphed into the conditional: 'I'm sorry if you were hurt by me suggesting you weren't really raped.'

Has also morphed into the bad-apple self-exculpation:'We're sorry our air bag knocked you unconscious and scarred your face but faulty air bags represent no more than .01 per cent of our product.'

Into the self-serving: 'We wish to apologise for the incident involving one of our staff whose behaviour fell below the standards on which we pride ourselves.'

And the euphemistic: 'We wish to express regret (regret is free-floating, sorry isn't) on the occasion of the recent incident involving accidental flawed proportions in our product (we poisoned you).'

A good apology is unconditional, direct, takes responsibility for the damage done (as opposed to the damage perceived by the injured party to have been done) registers how badly they were injured/offended, accepts that this injury or offence has done real and present damage to the injured or offended person, indicates determination to make it up to the person or people involved and confirms a firm purpose of amendment for the future. Last time you encountered one of them? Been a while, right? That's because when companies do things wrong, they pull together a lethal combination of lawyers who tell them they must not admit anything lest they get sued and PR people who want them to look on the bright side.

When medics make mistakes, killing or maiming patients, they don't even go to the PR people. They go straight to the lawyers, having first gone to considerable pains to avoid the injured patient or the relatives of the dead one. This inflicts at least six years of contentious bitterness on the already victimised, generates twice as much coverage and achieves damn all in the consequent court case.

Research indicates that when medics apologise straightforwardly in the immediate aftermath of a mistake, it minimises the chances of their being sued.

Apostrophe: A useful grammatical device, greatly misused by a generation of Irish people supposedly educated beyond levels ever achieved by their grandparents, who, in the main, did know how to use it.

Applause for pilots: Tends to happen after long flights, when a planeload of tourists break into hand-clapping as the plane taxies. Pilots despise this because it never reflects either the skill of the pilot or the complexity of the landing: bumpy landings in turbulence are often superbly handled in the cockpit but passengers tend to be too distracted by upchucking their appalling dinner/snack/breakfast in reaction to the 'rough air' to give proper validation to the person piloting the plane. Discriminatory, too. Nobody ever applauds the driver of the number 16 bus when he or she lands them at the terminal in one piece.

Aromatherapy: Medical excuse for buying sweet-smelling oils.

Art: Anything that has been created, invented, extruded, written, copied, stolen, found, slept in, excreted, recorded or destroyed by anyone regardless of their skill, its aesthetic worth or any discernible value. Now frequently accompanied by the verb 'to make'. Artists used to play, paint or sculpt. Now they 'make art'.

Artisanal: Appears to describe every single edible item for sale in a farmers' market. Ideally brown paper and twine are involved in packaging. The term is meant to convey the impression that the item is hand made by an artistic type in a hemp hut in the Burren. More likely to have been mass produced in a random factory in Ballyhaunis.

Artist: According to David Mamet: 'Once, almost in recent memory, a lower-class service (almost a menial job) the Arts have become, with the advent of mass media and the growth of the Superstar, a Helping Profession.

'Their status, and the status of their practitioners, has been raised. This has, of course, attracted quite a bit of riffraff to the arts. Folks who previously would have directed their efforts towards one of the other Protected Endeavors now call themselves artists. They do so because the arts offer the benefits of self proclaimability, supported by almost universal employment…"Video art" replaces film making, "Performance" replaces theatre, "Installations" replace sculpture."

Assertion: A statement of the unprovable, unsupported by evidence. Like: 'Runners are amazing. Running puts you more in control of your life.'

---

*   David Mamet, *Make-Believe Town: Essays and Remembrance*, New York: Little, Brown, 1996.

Untrue, both assertions. Runners are boring and develop skinny shoulders. Running irritates dogs, who take corrective action, costs a fortune because of the necessary gear and causes countless injuries and consequent surgery.

Assertiveness training: A lucrative method designed to help trainees of all genders and none to grow a pair.

As you do: 'I was falling from the plane at 20,000 feet, clutching a bowl of porridge, as you do…' The phrase is widely and wrongly believed to make funnier the main sentence to which it sticks like a barnacle. Believed to have first appeared in 1889, in Jerome K. Jerome's *Three Men in a Boat*, the usage was popularised by Eddie Izzard. One more reason not to read *Three Men in a Boat* or even think about Izzard.

Atherosclerosis: Fatty build-up in the arteries predisposing you to a heart attack. And it's your own fault. If you stopped eating doughnuts and chips and ate like our ancestors did, you'd be only grand. Or so we were told until two cardiologists looked at the arteries of King Merneptah, a pharaoh who lived 3200 years ago and, in his mummified state in the Al-Azhar university in Cairo, was hardly in a position to object to the intrusion. They found his arteries to be just as ropy as ours. 'I think there's something that we're missing,' said one of the cardiologists. You don't say…

Attention: The free gift each of us has the capacity to bestow on another. Every human being is born with an invisible sign, reading: 'Please find me interesting.' Most get a poor response throughout their lives.

At the end of the day: It's the night.

Awesome: Term veering into disrepute, as it is now used to describe anything vaguely positively or noteworthy. Its disuse welcomed, since it left the linguistically challenged singularly unprepared to describe any major natural disaster or beauty spot.

B

B-list: People in their forties and fifties whose career rope ran out a while back, so eager to get back on the celeb ladder that they will make fools of themselves in the background of reality shows as 'tutors'.

Baa, Baa, Bullshit: Journalist and broadcaster Ronan Casey's summing up of the laundering of nursery rhymes in order to make them fit 21st-century notions of what is acceptable, occasioned by the specific rewriting of 'Baa, Baa, black sheep' as 'Baa, baa, pink sheep'.

Baby talk: Don't knock it. That nonsense stuff mothers and fathers fill the ears of their babies with is hellish important. The more they're talked to, the better will be their eventual communication. Kill the mobile phone.

Bad: Good.

Badass: One who breaks societal norms. Not to be applied to steak, necklaces or hightops, which don't tend to challenge societal anything.

Bad choices: This is the great get-out-of jail card. Instead of admitting to doing evil things, villains now admit to having made bad choices. Bad choices and mistakes. A guy convicted of forty charges of rape, murder and arson sums it all up by saying, 'I've made mistakes.' To which the answer is: 'No, Sunshine, you made a mistake, singular. You got caught. Apart from that, everything you did was premeditated fully cognisant evil.' Or he confesses to having made bad choices. As if life was a dodgy buffet and he'd had the bad luck to pick the sushi that was past its best.

Bad driver: Garrison Keillor of the *Prairie Home Companion* radio series on National Public Radio maintains that all the children in Lake Wobegon, his fictional Lutheran town in middle America, are above average, which statisticians would believe to be impossible. However, evidence closer to home suggests that Ireland's cars are all driven by above-average drivers. Put it this way: can you remember the last time someone confessed to you that they were a bad driver? Occasionally – very occasionally – a woman may do so. A man, never.

A dearth of bad drivers means most drivers in this country are above average, which begs the question of what Liz O'Donnell and the RSA are for.

Bad news: We love it. Or rather, we hate it but we can't help concentrating on it. Thus, a blogger will focus, out of fifty-seven neutral or positive comments made by readers, on the two or three that are negative. It isn't just you: an American writer has pointed out the evolutionary reason behind us paying so much more attention to bad as opposed to good news. 'The explanation from evolutionary psychology,' says Paul Waldeman, 'is that looking out for danger was essential to survival (ignore a tasty raspberry bush and you'll go hungry for a day, ignore a sabre-toothed tiger and you won't be passing on your genes).'

Bail-out: A rescue provided by the rich to the poor. Widely misinterpreted as a method of imprisoning and humiliating nations that, without a bail-out, would have seen their civil servants walking the streets, jobless, their refuse uncollected and barter temporarily replacing commerce until full chaos took hold. One of the few words that has gone from a positive to a negative within a ten-year period.

Baking: Is the new tyranny. You have to bake cake, proffer cake, eat cake. Specifically, you have to make small continents of it with your children. Preferably your metrosexual boys, who know their way around the kitchen nearly as well as your girls know theirs around the rugby pitch.

The only – although as yet unstudied – good outcome of all this is that cake-baking may have an anti-depressant effect, if the experience of novelist Marian Keyes is anything to go by. Marian baked and baked when stricken by clinical depression and found it lifted her mood.

Banking enquiry: Uniquely Irish event, part of a uniquely Irish capacity to insist on setting up ineffectual investigations of past bad eggery while present bad eggery continues unabated. Resource- and time-intensive attempt to discover the cause of the banking collapse. Criticised by the public for its inability to hold those responsible to account despite said public having voted in referendum to deny Dáil committee that power. Itself potentially subject to enquiry.

Balance: A mythical concept attached to general elections and referenda like a fridge magnet and just as useful. Somebody in authority at some point decided that balance in an electoral situation meant 'equal time'. Giving Stephen Fry and a ninety-three-year-old car mechanic equal time on a television programme will tend somewhat to favour Stephen Fry. Giving protagonists of marriage equality (as in single sex marriage) and opponents thereof equal time, as happened coming up to the 2015 referendum, put the appearance of fairness on the programmed debates to which it applied.

This, of course, failed to take into account the tone and wording of questions directed to the anti-marriage-equality people, which ranged from the negative to the contemptuous.

It also failed to address the fact that the anti side, in this instance, was confined to a handful of people, the repetitious appearance of whom in itself could have skewed the delivery of balance, other than 'stopwatch balance', which was announced on the air by Marian Finucane and resented volubly, post factum, by Joe Duffy on the basis that it made life impossible on *Liveline* for the duration. Equal time on its own guarantees fairness to nobody and the concept needs revisitation by the broadcasting powers that be and the bodies that regulate the broadcasters.

Bald: A natural process affecting some men and a smaller number of women, together with cancer patients undergoing chemo. Joan Collins, bestselling author, said about her fiancé undergoing unsuccessful chemo: 'When he lost his black, thick curly hair, he didn't want to go on.'

While fatness has, throughout history, often been a sought-after look (and, trust us, it's easy to find and achieve) baldness never has. 'The comb-over goes back to ancient Rome, at least,' says hair-dressing archeologist Janet Stephens. 'Roman comb-overs were not based on the side part, as they are today. To part the hair was an exclusively feminine practice avoided by 'manly' Roman men. If a Roman's hair was thinning but still present, he allowed the hair at the crown to grow longer and combed it forward. This type of comb-over is visible on portrait statutes of Emperor Hadrian. If a man was Hippocratically bald [hairless on top, like the eponymous medic] he would grow any remaining hair longer and comb each side up over the top to meet in the middle.'

Ancient Romans who tried to thicken the appearance of their hair by inking their scalp were relentlessly mocked by the satirists of the day. Which goes to prove how painful baldness was then and is now and how cruel satirists could be, then and now. On the other hand, there's now the possibility of a hair transplant.

Bandwidth: Used by wannabe trendy business executives to indicate capacity: 'We wouldn't have the bandwidth to tackle that issue right now.'

Banter: Self-regarding term used by boys to describe shouted banalities.

Basically: Filler word, up there with 'definitely' and 'essentially'. Pads a meaningless sentence into an appearance of worth.

Battle royal: A conflict, not a dish. The 'royal' is not 'royale'.

Bear Grylls: An individual who goes where nobody else has ever gone, on his own, except for a production crew, to shout at animals and let on to be living like our ancestors did. At the last count, few of our ancestors had his support crew. Or his money. Or his fame. He represents the apotheosis of unreality TV.

Bed blocker: One of those insulting medical terms everybody condemns but for which no useful substitute exists. Meaning an older person whose presenting illness/injury has now been dealt with and who should be in a nursing home or in their own home with assistance but for whom such an option is not readily available.

Insulting medical terms first surfaced in *The House of God* by Samuel Shem, a pseudonym chosen by the author, himself a psychiatrist, whose real name was Stephen Bergman. 'When it comes to modern medical slang, there's Before Shem and After Shem,' says Brian Goldman. Goldman is something of an expert on the topic. He's spent thirty years as an emergency room physician in Toronto. He's written columns, delivered a TED talk that's been viewed more than a million times and recently published *The Secret Language of Doctors*, which cracks the code of hospital culture. Goldman maintains that Bergman shook the culture of modern medicine to its very foundation by introducing the public to a jarringly new kind of medical slang.

Begrudger: A participant in the national pastime of running down anyone or anything that seeks to get above its perceived station in life. As George III once observed: 'If you want to baste an Irishman you can easily get an Irishman to turn the spit.'

The late Brendan Behan was the main who nailed the first recorded begrudger in 1922. Ireland had just won its freedom and a priest remarked to the local blacksmith how marvellous this was. The blacksmith replied that with the gentry gone, he would lose business. The priest commented that we would soon have our own gentry. 'We will in our arse have our own gentry,' snapped the blacksmith, thereby starting a national pastime.

Hostilities were temporarily suspended during the Celtic Tiger years while we – briefly – celebrated figures like Seanie Fitzpatrick and let them lecture us about the nation spending too much on social welfare. The resumption of hostilities was slow, mainly because we realised that begrudging wasn't enough for the situation after the Celtic Tiger got mange, hoose and worms.

Belittling (others): How inadequates convince themselves they're adequate.

Big: Euphemism for fat.

Big arse: To be condemned when associated with a female politician. Ticket to fame for Kim Kardashian and J-Lo. Technical term: steatopygia, meaning the accumulation of fat on the buttocks, a normal condition in some African tribes.

Big data: Euphemism covering the reality that our every move, action and thought is being tracked by someone via our computers, mobile phones, tablets, credit cards, pacemakers, fitbit bracelets, biometric passports – among other things.

Big girl's blouse: A male wimp.

Big up: Exaggerate.

Bigotry: What anybody who disagrees with us displays.

Birthday: A constant challenge to the pronunciation abilities of broadcasters who can't hit the 'd', so it turns out 'Happy Birthay to you.'

Birthday party: A ritual which has attained status somewhere between a sacrament and a legal obligation, with penalty points for failure to invite the right children and provide them with the correct entertainment or requisite goody-bags.

Counter-obligations are laid upon the parents of the under-aged guests at these events. Both sides claim to resent these impositions.

Birth order: Like body language: everybody knows a bit of it, like that first-borns tend to be dominant, ambitious, conservative and jealous, whereas last-borns are more open and innovative. If you believe the research.

Bishop Brennan syndrome: Refers to an episode of *Father Ted,* wherein Ted kicks the eponymous bishop up the arse. The bishop is stunned by this assault and remains frozen in silence while he journeys to the Vatican to meet the Pope. Just as he is presented to His Holiness, the full realisation of what has happened to him strikes him and he announces to the Pontiff: 'That bollix kicked me up the arse.'

The same thing happened the population of Ireland when recession and cutbacks followed the explosive bursting of the property bubble. They absorbed the consequent punishment in relative silence for two or three years. Then a catalyst named Irish Water unglued them and put them on the streets, protesting. But what they were really saying was: 'Those bollixes [in government] kicked us up the arse.'

Blaa: A soft round floppy type of bread associated with Waterford. Someone applied to Europe to have it recognised as a regional delicacy and kept a straight face when they succeeded.

Blanking: Cutting people dead. If you want to do it live on a TV programme, gaze fixedly at the bridge of the other person's nose. Everybody else thinks you're looking at them but it makes them miserably uncomfortable.

Blue sky thinking: Management bullshit term, up there with the 'big hairy idea' when it comes to stating the bleeding obvious in what the speaker believes to be a brand new term. It never is.

Board member: Prominent retired businessman. Prominent retired businesswomen, instead of being asked to go on boards where they would be paid, are invited to mentor younger businesswomen. For free.

Body: What's left went someone dies. Or passes. Often replaced in media reports with the repulsive 'remains.'

BOGOF: Buy one, get one free. Marketing device that became popular during the recession years.

Bog snorkelling: Idiot pastime dreamed up by people with more time than sense.

Bog standard home: One with a swimming pool, tennis court, view of the sea and copious accommodation within which to plan continued occupation by a family convinced of their modest lifestyle despite owing banks seventy million.

Boho chic: A whatever-you're-having-yourself fashion mix made up of references to everything from gypsy gear to hippy flowers. Lots of floaty skirts, lacy fastenings and flying ribbons. Unsuited to anyone over twenty-three. Unsuited to men.

Book: The demise of the book has falsely been predicted a number of times. The demise of the book as we know it was falsely predicted with the advent of the Kindle, which, with its ability to store a small library and offer bookmarks and definitions at will, was clearly so much better than the old assembly of pages between hard or soft covers that the latter would die off within the decade. It didn't and hardy old hardbacks and less hardy old paperbacks continued to sell. Nor will the traditional book die out, according to Professor John Sutherland of University College London, who for no good reason has reduced twenty-five famous novels to 140 character tweets but who seems sensible otherwise.

Despite all the predictions that Twitter and Facebook will kill off the book, Sutherland says that both apps are a time-limited aspect of growing up and no more than that. Young people, he says, like horses in a field, want to cluster and rub up against each other and that, in effect, is what they do electronically. 'As you get older,' he adds, 'privacy becomes more important.'

Which is one of the reasons why books retain their hold. Frequent fliers, for example, know that opening a book is a great way to discourage the passenger in the next seat from seeking to engage in conversation. Plus the book has a capacity to transport its reader to another time and another place and to facilitate the meeting of characters who – let's be honest – are a whole load more interesting than the real people we meet every day.

The genre most successfully making nonsense out of the recurring Cassandra-isms is the children's book. The number of titles aimed at children doubled between 2014 and 2015, according to the annual list compiled by *The Bookseller,* the trade magazine, the editor of which says: 'Children's books are really, really strong.'

Booker: The all-powerful researcher who books guests for programmes. He or she has to have the tenacity of a barnacle, the versatility of a chameleon, the determination of General Sherman and his willingness to burn to the ground any obstacle in the way, the charm of Colin Farrell and a religious devotion to the success of the presenter.

The craft is at its most advanced (if that's the correct term) in the US, where Brian Stelter's book about morning television describes it thus: 'If the bookers have any shame, they have suppressed it. They will drop off homemade cookies and handwritten notes on a crime victim's front porch. They'll take campaign strategists out to dinner and get them drunk. They'll flirt, cajole, cry, beg and their bosses don't want to know what else, because they believe ratings and their own paychecks are at stake. (The bookers at ABC barely flinched when one of their own bragged of sleeping with an adult witness in a child abuse trial to secure an interview.)'*

Boredom: Scientifically established as one of the great workplace stressers.

Boyfriend: Precursor to lover, partner and husband. Acceptable in teenagers. Ridiculous in those over fifty. Ditto 'girlfriend'.

Brainstorming: When a group of people sit in a room, with their phones ostentatiously on 'meeting'. Those whose brains are worth

---

*   Brian Stelter, *Top of the Morning*, New York: Grand Central Publishing, 2013.

storming are thinking about all the work they could be doing instead of being physically present for this shite and feel like complete plonkers.

Someone present does a mapping exercise which looks like a badly-built bird's nest and those whose brains never move beyond the banal describe it as 'blue sky thinking' or as having got everybody 'outside the box', neither of which, if meaningful, would be true.

Brainstorming does, however, have one benefit. It figures in 360 degree feedback of bosses as a positive, indicative of their willingness to listen to the lower orders. This isn't true either.

Brave: Virtue attributed to anybody revealing something about themselves that speaks fearlessly into the liberal consensus. Surviving right-wingers and fundamentalists, when they open their mouths to oppose said consensus, are never so described.

Break the internet: Successor to 'went viral'. Used by online 'content specialists' to describe any picture or article with more than two hundred likes.

Breaking silence: Headlines indicating that a celeb who hasn't said anything about a particular scandal for at least two hours has now tweeted about it.

Breastfeeding: It must stop, according to Radio Solent DJ Alex Dyke. At least in public. Only 'librarian-type, moustachioed' women do it anyway and the only men who don't object to it are wimps. He has further opined that a yummy mummy wouldn't do it because a yummy mummy would know it's not a good look and anyway formula is just as good.

This discourse could have gone on and on, had the Beeb not stepped in and suspended him, no doubt aware that the NHS says that babies should be breastfed for at least six months because it has such marked advantages for the little sprout over formula.

Bridge: An engineering miracle adopted by gobshites in recent years, said gobshites ruining the look of some of the most beautiful examples by locking padlocks on to them and endangering, by the accumulated weight, the structure of the bridge.

Also a card game of which the late Omar Sharif was the star exponent. Bridge is a little-appreciated cesspit of marital infidelity at an orderly decent level.

Brompton: The elite of folding bikes.

Brompton cocktail: So named because it was developed in London's Brompton Hospital in the first quarter of the 20th century for the treatment of patients suffering from terminal cancer. It comprised morphine (to manage pain), cocaine (to keep the patient awake and cheery), chlorpromazine, 90 per cent alcohol and flavoured syrup. Doctors of an older generation believed in it with a passion as allowing patients to spend meaningful and reasonably happy and lucid time with their family before dying. (The same doctors tended to have a lot of faith in morphine, which, in and of itself, suppressed not only pain but breathing, which tended to write *finis* to the patient's life.) The Brompton cocktail has been discontinued. Pity.

Brown paper bags: A specifically Irish term for corruption, meaning the delivery of untraceable cash in unmarked paper bags. It is generally assumed that because of codes of ethics and the presence of a million regulators, the habit has passed and the nation is now clean. Watch this space.

Bucket list: In 2007 they made an eponymous film, starring Jack Nicholson and Morgan Freeman, playing a billionaire and a car mechanic who find themselves side by side in hospital beds with bad diagnoses. This is clearly fiction. Bad diagnoses are class-blind. Hospital beds are not.

However, this odd couple, in order to find out who they really are (you'd think they'd know by that age, although forgetting is always a possibility) leave their hospital beds to have experiences and a final adventure before they die. Other movies have been made about the same theme: what the central character must do or see before they kick the bucket.

The phrase 'kick the bucket' goes back to mediaeval hangings, when the perpetrator was put standing on a bucket while the noose was affixed around his or her neck, a swift kick then removing the bucket and relatives and friends leaping into action to hang on to the perp's legs in order to quicken his or her departure from this life.

According to *Slate* magazine, 'In 2004, the term was used – perhaps for the first time? – in the context of things to do before one kicks the bucket (a phrase in use since at least 1785) in Patrick M. Carlisle's book *Unfair & Unbalanced: The Lunatic Magniloquence of Henry E. Panky.*'

Bugle-style: Drinking straight from the bottle. As an adult. Supposedly.

Burglar: Lads who break into the homes of people who are at funerals and weddings in order to nick their stuff. 75 per cent of burglaries in Ireland are committed by 25 per cent of burglars. Which suggests it may be habit-forming.

Byebyebyebyebye: A deeply irritating parting song sung on mobile phone calls for no sensible reason.

C

Call: This is an odd one. Increasingly, it's being said, when describing an incident, that 'a woman called Nelly O'Sullivan' or 'a man called Jeremiah Byrne' was involved. Untrue. A woman named Nelly O'Sullivan, or a man named Jeremiah Byrne was involved. Unless each of them operates under an alias. Or has been given a permanent description like 'the General'. Nelly could be called the bitch from hell and Jeremiah could be called or known as the meanest man in Roscrea but neither is their name.

Call out: To reprove, reproach, contradict or berate in the noisiest possible way. The *Daily Beast* reported: 'Nicki Minaj Calls Out Miley at VMAS. Bang! A clearly furious Nicki Minaj called Miley Cyrus a "bitch" live on stage for comments she had made about her in *The New York Times* during MTV's Video Music Awards on Sunday night. "And now back to this bitch that had a lot to say about me the other day in the press," Minaj said when accepting her award, pointing at Cyrus, who was hosting the ceremony.'

Candidate: Eddie Hobbs. For Renua. Or then again, maybe not. Perhaps. Who knows?

Car boot sale: This phenomenon had just begun to take off when eBay arrived and it was widely assumed that eBay would kill it off. However, the recession gave it legs, if not wheels, and it is now a cherished part of Irish life.

Carceral society: Description applied to the US because it loves prisons.

Careful: Irish for 'mean'.

Cat videos: The true reason the internet was invented. Arguably the most visited sites on the web, cat videos showing cute kittens raise the international mood on a daily basis.

However, the one really worth watching is of Christian the lion. This is a rediscovered dead lion. We assumed it to be dead, given the survival-to-old-age limitations of life in the jungle.

Not that Christian the lion started in a jungle. He started in Harrods, where, in the 1960s, incredible as it may seem, it was possible to buy lion cubs. Two guys bought Christian as a pet. A few years later, they realised that keeping a nearly full-grown lion in a city was not acceptable and transported theirs to the jungle, where he was gradually reintroduced to the wild, to which he adjusted pretty well. (The fact that he could manage in the wild, paradoxically, meant he would have a shorter life. Lions live much longer in zoos than they do in the wild.) A year later, his two former owners decided to holiday in Kenya and take their chances on seeing Christian. They waited in the location where he had last been spotted, and eventually, as one of them wrote to his parents the next day, Christian appeared about seventy-five yards distant from them.

'He stared hard at us for a few seconds, and then slowly moved closer for a good look. He stared intently. He looked marvellous, and up on the rocks, he didn't appear much bigger. We couldn't wait any longer and called him. He immediately started to run down towards us. Grunting with excitement, this enormous lion jumped all over us, but he was very gentle.'

The letter doesn't begin to do justice to the reunion between men and lion. The grainy film, on the other hand, does. The lion hugs the two of them with a passion, muzzling his head into their necks, bounding from one to the other.

Nearly forty years after the reunion, someone put footage of the encounter up on YouTube and the two men, one of them now an art curator, one a wildlife expert, began to hear from people who had seen the video and been profoundly moved by it. TV programmes picked up on the story. A publisher decided to update and re-release *A Lion Called Christian*, the book the two men had written about their lion in 1971.

If the weather isn't great where you are today, or if you're bored or lonely, go on the internet and type in 'lion reunion'. No matter which version you land on, it will hardly take a minute of your time.

But the footage of a hugely powerful animal delivering ecstatic affection to two returned friends will warm your heart in a way small cat videos cannot. We don't know why – and neither do the two men, now in their sixties. It just will. Trust us.

Catastrophilia: The craving for danger which is the first necessary trait of the journalist.

Catfishing: Online dating scam predicated on the desperation of the target. An elaborate system of 'outing' the catfisher has been developed, which requires the target to ask the suspected catfisher to take a picture of themselves with that day's newspaper in the shot, in order to establish their real age or even their existence.

Suggestion: if you have to go to that much trouble to make sure that the person seeking to date you is not just after your money, looking more positively at the people you work and socialise with might be a better option.

Catwalk diversity: Where fashion opens its big events to women who do not meet the model norm because they are shorter, fatter or carry a disability. Always being promised. Never going to happen in an other than token way.

Celebrity: Someone who is famous for no particular reason.

Celtic phoenix: Wishful language used to describe Ireland's economic recovery. Ordinary humans (as opposed to media professionals and politicians) never use it. They know better.

Censorship: A sweet old concept. We may still have a Censorship of Publications Board that works hard to prevent us being polluted by what we read. As long as we read only books. Back in 1954, more than a thousand books were banned. No book has been banned in Ireland since 1998.

How it works is that some puritan zealot complains to the board suggesting that a given book is obscene, indecent, or promulgates an illegal act.

The board reads the possibly offensive book and decides whether or not it should be taken off the market. The most recent example was the reissue of *Laura*, a novel written by Alan Shatter about ministers having affairs. (This was written before Mr Shatter became a minister.) The board didn't ban its reissue.

Change agents: Usually self-claimed by people with meaningless jobs in big corporations. Real change agents are unmistakable. Think Lehman Brothers.

Channel: To display or copy the characteristics or appearance of someone else or of another time. As in: 'Miranda Kerr channels the 1970s in a blue peasant dress and fringed bag.'

Charm: The capacity to convince others that one is happy out when in fact one is bored rigid.

Cheating: In marital terms, widely distributed in Ireland, as evidenced by the hacking of the Ashley Madison website, which was devoted to facilitating affairs.

More than 100,000 Irish people had subscribed to the site, with email addresses revealing that cheats are to be found working for RTÉ, banks, the civil service, the HSE, An Garda Síochána, the Defence Forces and academia. The geographical distribution was equally fair-minded, although with an understandable concentration in Dublin.

Checklist: Vital to health, safety and survival. Charles Lindbergh's son maintains that the biggest contribution his father made to aviation wasn't the flight on the *Spirit of St Louis* but the safety checklist. 'As a pilot,' Reeve Lindbergh writes, 'my father habitually kept comprehensive lists on all his equipment and all his flying procedures.

'He checked and rechecked these constantly to make sure that everything he did before, during and after each flight was appropriate and that the aircraft was kept in top condition.'

The aviation checklist was further developed before the Second World War, when a test plane was discontinued because of crashes due to pilot error, with the newspapers of the time describing the Boeing aircraft as 'too much airplane for one man to fly'. Boeing nearly went bankrupt as a result.

But some of the test pilots had faith in the plane and came up with an ingeniously simple approach: a pilot's checklist, because 'flying this new plane was too complicated to be left to the memory of any one person, however expert.'[*]

---

[*]   Reeve Lindbergh, *Beneath a Wing*, Dublin: Poolbeg Press, 2000.

The plane flew and the checklist became more deeply embedded in aviation history. Now the man who leads the World Health Organization's Safe Surgery Saves Lives programme, Dr Atul Gawande, argues that checklists – specifically a ninety-second checklist proven to reduce deaths and complications – should be applied to the varied and complex world of surgery.

Chefs: Self-publicists without shame, ubiquitous throughout the media, 90 per cent of them eager to prove that they're not screaming violent divas and unwilling to admit it was the screaming violent divas that got the profession where it is today.

Chemistry (lack of): The excuse used when a male TV personality doesn't want to work with a female TV personality.

Chicklit: Term of derision. Roundly deserved by fiction devoted to shopping and shagging. Applied to almost everything written by women other than a narrow band of work validated as high literature. No male equivalent.

Child-abuser statue: If we have to choose between statues in Dublin's most important street, how about we keep the anti-alcohol monk and lose the child abuser?

The choice is being forced upon us by the LUAS. In order to let the LUAS go where no LUAS has gone before, the 124-year-old statue of Fr Mathew, the man who invented the 'pledge', is being uprooted. For good. Or for evil, if you are enthusiastic about Fr Mathew's contribution to Irish life. The statue portrays a slender monk with wavy hair, a rosary beads and one of those rope belts, gesturing in an ambivalent way. One hand could be interpreted as him calling the barman for a round, the other, palm down at waist level, looks like he's asking everybody to keep the noise down.

The Railway Procurement Agency is in active discussions with someone in order to find a new home for Fr Mathew. Perhaps those active discussions might include the possibility of removing the child molester from O'Connell Street and substituting the temperance priest.

The child molester is – or was – William Smith O'Brien, one of the leaders of the Young Irelanders in the 19th century. You'd know by the statue he was born into privilege, getting his education in Harrow and TCD. Buying first into the nationalist cause and then into violent promulgation of the nationalist cause, he became involved in the inefficient, ineffective and frankly ridiculous 1848 rebellion. As a result, he was sentenced to death for treason but – the British authorities having more savvy in the 19th century than they did in the early 20th, had his sentence commuted to deportation to Van Diemen's Land.

So off our young hero goes to Van Diemen's Land, leaving his wife and several children behind him in Ireland. As it turned out, Van Diemen's Land wasn't actually so bad. He had a little house to himself in what constituted an open prison with a pleasant climate and Sergeant Kevin Lapham from Kildare in charge of him. Lapham was younger than Smith O'Brien and broadminded in his interpretation of what constituted state incarceration, taking him on scenic tours and treated him as something of a celeb.

The only thing he couldn't do for him was allow him to post letters without those letters being read for evidence of sedition. This diktat covered letters to Mrs Smith O'Brien, back in Ireland with the kids and very mean and sad it was, as diktats go. It might be assumed that Mr Smith O'Brien would shrug, decide that all he needed to do was keep his letters clean of rebellious incitement and all would be well. That assumption would be wrong, because this was a principled man who simply downed his quill and refused to write to his wife at all. For ten years, he maintained his principled silence.

Which may not have been that unwelcome to Mrs Smith O'Brien, who was used to letters from her husband, back in the day when he was in Ireland, ticking her off for wanting him at home doing child-minding when he had to be off saving Ireland from the oppressor.

If William Smith O'Brien had shortcomings as a revolutionary and husband, they were as nothing in comparison to his shortcomings as a friend and beneficiary of Lapham's kindness. Two police officers used a telescope to get the evidence which must have destroyed Lapham's life: of Smith O'Brien being sexually serviced by Lapham's thirteen-year-old daughter. They got busy with the telescope because they had seen him kissing the child on more than one occasion in a way that jarred with them. Their evidence changed how Smith O'Brien was imprisoned from then on and he obliquely referred to it in his diary, excusing himself (of course) by reference to the frailties of human nature.

If we've a choice between a man who recognised an endemic problem – alcohol abuse – and created a method to put solidarity around sobriety and a man who lectured and later ignored his wife for ten years and who then, despite being married and despite the kindness of her father, sexually exploited a thirteen-year-old, Fr Mathew looks like a keeper, rather than Smith O'Brien.

Chillax: An invitation to relax and calm down which never worked, as an invitation or as a term. Now as good as dead.

Chugger: The poor unfortunate who civilly approaches passersby in a busy street, seeking to get them to sign a contract committing them to ongoing contribution to some charity. The word is a portmanteau term, pulling together 'charity' and 'mugger' and became amazingly popular and well understood directly after its introduction. Some Irish charities depend for up to one third of their income on the donors persuaded by chuggers. Strict rules govern how chuggers operate. The mistake many people make when accosted is that they don't say, 'Thank you, no,' and keep walking. Instead, they get involved in conversations they don't want to have, commit to what they don't want to commit to, then blame the chugger.

Clickbait: When a link, typically on Facebook or Twitter, has a sensational and/or engaging title to seduce you to click it through to a website whose content leaves you disappointed and angry. (Usually contains a reference to someone named Kardashian.)

Climate change: Something we all care about. Passionately. It ranks in sixteenth place among the things about which we care — passionately — and will do something about some time. As long as it doesn't involve giving up driving or flying or staying warm in winter.

Climate justice: What started out as global warming and should have stayed that way. It morphed into the infinitely duller and less threatening climate change just as sensible people began to realise that global warming was not a good thing and had downstream implications like drowning (if you live on an island) or malaria (if you live in west Cork, because the mosquitoes are on their way north). The most recent rendition, loved by NGOs, is climate justice, because those NGOs know that climate change greatly contributes to mass migration in the form of huge tides of homeless, stateless peoples. They also know that climate change leads to ever more unjust distribution of water and that it disproportionately screws up the lives of the poor, right across the world.

Clinton time: Term devised by Bill Clinton's aides to cover him always being an hour or two behind schedule. One commentator observed that when it came to unpunctuality, Clinton was an equal opportunities offender: 'He could be as late for a meeting with high-rolling executives as for one with poor farmers.'

Most Irish government ministers, of all parties, run on Clinton time.

Cockroach: A much maligned insect of the beetle kind, distinguished by its survival capacities, largely derived from having radar in its arse.

Coffee snobbery: Coffee snobbery went on the march in the last few years. Rightly so, up to a point. Some of us remember when offices kept a bulb of pre-made coffee warm on a hotplate for hour after hour, so that someone desperate for a quick jolt of caffeine would find themselves getting outside a beverage that had the consistency of chicken stock and delivered the sensory thrill of barely liquid creosote. The horror of old-time coffee of this kind wasn't just attributable to its longevity: the limitations on the types of ground coffee available contributed too.

Then coffee shops took a quantum leap into taste and retrained everybody's palate. Within a couple of years, everybody knew about Arabica and bought bags of ground coffee with descriptions on the front of the packet which promised 'undercurrents of blackcurrant and honey with light touches of wheatgrass and spaghetti'. To offer a visitor a cup of instant coffee became a crime against nature and to be told you brewed 'great coffee' was like being awarded an Emmy.

The downside was that everybody felt they had to get that Emmy and those peddling coffee made the brewing of the beverage seem more challenging than earning a doctorate in theoretical physics. Now, between you, me and that chipped mug over there, making great coffee is as simple as boiling an egg, if not simpler. You don't need a machine that looks like an antique train with small metal cups into which to stuff ground coffee and little appendages to steam the milk. A cone of filter paper, a couple of spoonfuls of coffee and you're good to go. If you run out of filter paper, kitchen roll makes a perfectly functional substitute.

That said, fear of coffee-making inadequacy created a powerful market for manufacturers of machines which required the owner to deploy only water, electricity and a pod. Like printer manufacturers who could charge half nothing for their machines in order to generate a semi-permanent market for inkjet cartridges, businesses like Keurig were setting themselves up for continuous selling of pods.

The K-pod business model is based on the assumption that, once they have hooked the customer, that customer can be expected to spend about fifty Euro per pound on the coffee contained in the K-Cups, five times the cost of even gourmet ground coffee bought in the bag. That's an awful lot of money to spend to get around your coffee-making incompetence.

The K-pod people had their customers by the short and curlies. Until they went too far, as tends to happen businesses that believe they have their customers by the short and curlies. Up to a certain point, the company had provided reusable cups the customer could refill from any coffee bag, thus meeting the needs of both the overpaid stupid and the underpaid sensible coffee drinkers. But then they got greedy and decided to force the underpaid sensible coffee drinkers to line up behind the rich dopes. They brought out a new machine incompatible with the self-filling pods. It was also incompatible with earlier pods, which seriously annoyed loyal customers. Their annoyance was nothing compared to the fury of the lads who had been filling their own pods with their own coffee.

In tandem with the customer rage came competitor opportunism. Fair dues to them, a family company named Rogers came up with a clip that could be affixed to any pod – including the infinitely reusable pod – which would fool the new Keurig machine into thinking it was dealing with the new Keurig pod. The Rogers people sold this with the slogan: 'Go forth and brew in freedom.'

This perfect consumer storm caused the sales of Keurig machines to tank. They dropped by nearly a quarter. They may have been on the point of market saturation anyway but the coincidence of the failure to force-sell the new machine and the hostile coverage generated by customers who were mad as hell resulted in a 10 per cent drop in the share value of the company.

This was when the penny dropped and, as the *Washington Post* put it, the company K-pitulated. It apologised to everybody and promised a firm purpose of amendment. Specifically, Keurig will teach their new machines to appreciate diversity and to embrace refillable pods without prejudice.

Anyone for a cup of corporate contrition?

Coital migraine: Galen, a Greek medic working of the 2nd century BC, maintained: '*Post coitum omne animal triste est, sive gallus et mulier.*' Why he said it in Latin, we're not sure. But in English, his dictum is: 'All animals are sad after sex, except cocks and women.' Let's not argue that one, shall we?

On the other hand, sufferers from coital migraine are seriously sad after sex, because they experience blinding head pain. They should consider Botox injections. Not that we're making medical re-commendations but one of the odd spin-offs of Botox is its capacity to reduce the frequency of this vicious form of headache. (Like flu and allergies, migraine is subject to medical inflation. Folks with a mild pain in their heads claim migraine, much to the fury of genuine sufferers.)

Colouring: Euphemism for 'having sex' in use in front of small children, to allow their parents to set up a play date for later and matching anticipation, without talking dirty.

Comfortable in his/her skin: Recurring description of any reasonably integrated individual. Who the hell else's skin would anybody be comfortable in?

Complain: What the rich don't do, according to a man who claims to be a self-made millionaire. T. Harv Eker says complaining is the worst thing you can do for your health or career. (To which we would add that it doesn't improve your social life, either.) Eker says that if you're in a career rut, the first thing you should do is shut the hell up about your hard times and the evil ones who are causing them. Not only in conversation but inside your own head.

Compensation: The first time an Irish person hears this to describe their salary from their American multinational employer, they are floored, having grown up with 'compensation' as a term to describe money conned out of an insurance company on a claim of whiplash made by a relative who wouldn't know whiplash if it bit them in the arse, which, anatomically, might be difficult.

Complement: Little understood term, meaning to contribute or add to. Custard complements rhubarb crumble. It doesn't compliment it.

Compliment: Word frequently confused with 'complement', meaning to flatter or praise someone. Nobody in Ireland knows how to pay a compliment. 'Gosh, you look great and that colour really suits you,' is a compliment. 'Skinny bitch, I hate you,' is kind of a compliment. 'Where did you buy the dress?' is not a compliment.

Cognitive behaviour therapy: One of the most effective approaches to mental troubles. Short-term and effective, it is the alternative to, *inter alia,* the old psychoanalysis which saw patients lying on a couch in the therapist's office for months, years or decades, talking randomly about aspects of their childhood in order to come to an understanding of what got them to where they are. (On the couch, with a silent therapist at a right angle at the head of the couch.) Some forms of cognitive-behaviour treatments (CBT) are used to combat post-traumatic stress disorder (PTSD), while others systematically desensitise those who suffer from phobias. CBT includes stress inoculation training, cognitive processing therapy, cognitive therapy, assertiveness training, biofeedback and relaxation training, in addition to combinations of several different modalities. In contrast to older talk therapies CBT techniques last a shorter time, sometimes achieving the objective in half a dozen to a dozen narrowly-spaced sessions, meeting once or twice a week. CBT focuses on the present and on skills to cope with problems like panic attacks, rather than on worrying about the historic roots of the problem.

Cognitive dissonance: F. Scott Fitzgerald defined 'genius' as the ability to hold two mutually contradictory thoughts in your head at one and the same time. For most people this adds up to cognitive dissonance, which can be confusing and stressful. The former finance minister (briefly) of Greece, Yanis Varoufakis, maintained that obeying the rules of the bailout whereby Greece was handed €86bn in rescue funds created cognitive dissonance among his fellow politicians: 'For it is clear that once you start implementing policies it becomes untenable to say constantly, "I am passing law X through parliament even though I think it is toxic."

'At some point either you resign or you remove the cognitive dissonance by beginning to believe that law X ain't that bad; perhaps that is what the doctor ordered.'

Varoufakis created global cognitive dissonance after his resignation from the Greek government, when he zoomed off on a motorcycle, quite properly wearing a protective helmet. His wife, sitting on the pillion behind him, was, however, bareheaded. Duty of marital care, anyone?

Combative: The ultimate survival tool, widely misinterpreted as having an extra syllable. It doesn't. One 'T' will do.

Comeback: What any current diva is described as doing after a month's layoff.

Commence: According to journalist Kevin Myers, the giveaway that nothing is ever going to happen, when included in a policy statement. Myers's theory is that when governments or agents of public policy genuinely set out to achieve something, they talk more simply of 'beginning'.

Committee member: A GAA equivalent of the rugby alickadoo. Controls parking, discipline and occasionally still plays at junior level. Junior hurler also applies.

Competence: An essential but increasingly rare career attribute that has largely been replaced with unfounded claims to be passionate, highly motivated, innovative, self-starting team players.

Complacency: A dangerous attitude ministers warn us against in their speeches. Except coming up to elections, perhaps because complacency doesn't rank high up in the list of expressed emotions they encounter on the doorstep.

Complaints: Customers may not tell you that they are unhappy with your service but surveys by the US Office of Consumer Affairs reveal that while 5 per cent of customers who are unhappy may complain to the company involved, the silent majority would rather switch than fight, so they take their money elsewhere. But they are unlikely to remain silent. Prior to the internet, a dissatisfied customer would tell between ten and twenty other people. Now they complain about hotels to hotel complaint sites and about doctors to relevant sites and Facebook the hell out of the issue. Their friends and followers multiply the effect almost to infinity.

Compliance: A substitute for virtue. It doesn't matter if you do a great job. In the compliance culture, all that matters is that you can tick the boxes on the compliance form.

Composite likeness: Increasingly sophisticated development of photographic likenesses of dead victims of crime or of suspects, the most breathtakingly successful of which was Baby Doe, a life-like photograph developed from the decomposed body of a four-year-old found in a black plastic bag which so resembled the toddler in life that its widespread publication in the US led to the arrest of the child's mother and the mother's boyfriend.

Con Air syndrome: The syndrome whereby you own a DVD of a movie – like *Con Air* – and never take it down from the shelf but the minute you see it coming up on television, you say, 'Oh, great,' and settle in with relish to watch it.

Conference ambassador: Conferences, congresses, annual general whatevers are part of the bright future of Irish tourism. It starts with the decision to locate an organisation's major coming-together in Ireland in a particular year. As soon as that decision is made, all those who might be persuaded to attend get battered with information, not just about the academic heavyweights who will speak to the gathered group but about the location and the delight-ful leisure pursuits awaiting participants when they drag themselves away from the tough work of listening, learning and debating.

Conferences and congresses may be worth three times the value of leisure tourism to the economy. We're all delighted to welcome backpackers from Sweden and coach tourists from the USA but several hundred orthopaedic surgeons or forklift drivers coming here for their annual knees-up has a more beneficial economic impact.

The fascinating aspect of this is how many people, worldwide, join organisations or societies or associations related to their profession, sport, business or obsession, creating structures for contact and an almost inevitable desire to get together once a year to celebrate being Parrot Heads or UFO-watchers or kettle-bell swingers.

Businesses making stents, circus performers doing stunts and climatologists worrying in a scientific way about weather all add up to a growing market.

It's a unique market, in that it can only be sold to by people who aren't tourism professionals. They're called conference ambassadors.

One could be a mother who, having given birth to twins, joined a global multiple birth organisation. As a 'conference ambassador', she may try to bring its annual conference here. Or it could be a vet, an archaeologist, a remote-control airplane flier or a naturist.

If you'd fancy being such a conference ambassador, Fáilte Ireland would love to help you bring your group's annual conference to Ireland. Even your oddball obsession could bring business to this country. As long as it's legal, of course. Which naturism is. When you pick the right location.

Conniption: First used in the US in the mid-19th century to describe a hysterically negative reaction: 'If you don't come in here this minute, I swear I shall have a conniption fit.' In Ireland, the 'fit' bit has been amputated and conniptions are rarely had on their own. Like the troubles to which they respond, they are plural: 'I was trying to explain that it didn't work that way but she was having conniptions and paying no attention to me.' Domestic conniption-causers are leaving the toilet seat up and failing to remember someone's birthday.

This is not to suggest that women are more given to conniptions than men, although men would make that claim, which is enough to give anyone of any gender a conniption.

Conscience: The key to honorable living is having a conscience that cannot be eroded by peer pressure.

'Just remember that one thing does not abide by majority rule, Scout – it's your conscience.' Atticus Finch in *To Kill a Mockingbird*.

Consultant: Term shared by highly paid hospital specialists with individuals on Linkedin filling in with freelance jobs while they seek full-time employment.

Control freak: What control freaks call normal people. Projection.

Control by kindness: Irish syndrome whereby people, often relatives, give you the shirt off your back, complete with instructions on how to wear it. And wash it. And iron it. Even if you didn't want the shirt in the first place.

Conventional wisdom: How conventional wisdom is born, according to the American lawyer who defended Imelda Marcos, Gerry Spence: 'a roomful of reporters and TV anchorpersons interviewing each other in the hallway at recesses, forming their consensus. Then the talking people rush back and tell it to the listening public in those short soundbites and…suddenly we have a national consensus.'*

Conversation: Substitute for vision suggested by politicians like Hillary Clinton. Public invitations to 'join the conversation' are issued by those who get money out of your texts or tweets.

Courage: Political, military and business leaders have to have it under pressure: 'For if the trumpet give an uncertain sound, who shall prepare himself to the battle?' 1 *Corinthians* 14.5.

Corporate contrition: Used to be rare; now, thanks to Oireachtas committees and the banking enquiry, frequent. The format is uniform: the banker/former minister/former Taoiseach says sorry for any suffering that happened but fails to take any blame for causing it.

'Coached contrition,' according to *Sunday Times* columnist Justine McCarthy, 'has become the default for corporations and the state when caught red-handed. Say sorry and move on.'

---

*   Gerry Spence, *O.J. The Last Word*, New York: St Martin's Press, 1997.

Coolidge effect: Male rats completely exhausted from copulation will become active again when new females are introduced into their environment, according to Peggy Vaughan.*

Crapulous: The behaviour that has caused the obesity epidemic. Eating and drinking too much. Way too much.

Credentialism: Reliance on academic degrees rather than ability. If a fool does an MBA, the end result is an overeducated fool who should, thereafter, stay in college and do a doctorate. Less dangerous to the rest of us.

Credit card: The little plastic enemy of your solvency.

Credit snatcher: The person in every office who claims to be the one who started anything worthwhile. Often believed and rewarded by their boss. Always hated by their peers, who, with justification, lie in the long grass praying for the chance to stick it to the credit snatcher.

Crowdfunding: Last resort of wannabe entrepreneurs who want to start a business nobody wants to fund, so they try to get everybody to fund them.

Crowdsource: An over-rated supposed method of persuading total strangers to fund an individual requiring a therapy for which the state will not stump up.

Crushed hate: The cause of Irish melancholy according to Shane Leslie, the writer and diplomat.

---

*   Peggy Vaughan, *The Monogamy Myth*, Newmarket Press, 1989.

Crying: 'There's no crying in baseball,' according to *A League of Their Own*, the 1992 film about the fictional formation of an all-girl professional baseball league during the Second World War.

Said in desperation by the character played by Tom Hanks when one of the young women he was coaching wept in response to criticism.

Women in any business should adopt their own variant:

– 'There's no crying in politics.'
– 'There's no crying in the office.'

Cuckoo in the nest: A phrase which needs reviving, if only to register that some things in nature are born evil. The cuckoo is a serial killer. Female cuckoos can't be bothered building a nest, so they lay their eggs in other birds' nests – one per nest – and feck right off. When the cuckoo egg hatches, the emerging blind bird has no relationship to the other birds and proves it immediately. It has a hollow in its back, all the better to scoop up round objects like the other bird's eggs, which it turfs over the edge of the nest.

Culture: Anything you decide is culture. Especially if you can get it sponsored by the Arts Council. Even a roller derby can be cultural.

Culture of complaint: Phrase dreamed up by art critic and historian Robert Hughes. Greatly fostered by radio phone-in programmes, which are as diet-dependent on complaint as a koala is on eucalyptus. (Koalas, which should not be described as 'bears' because it is tautologous, are cute but thick as planks.)

Cupcake: The grey squirrel of baking. Just as the grey knocked hell out of the native and prettier red squirrel and almost made it extinct, so the cupcake has knocked hell out of the fairy cake. Our grandparents would mourn.

Curate: As a noun, describes a dying breed: the local priest. Currently being replaced without fanfare by women of advanced years and faith.

As a verb, it is a misbegotten lump of pretentiousness. Curators used to work at museums, although they rarely described themselves as 'curating' the collections of which they took care.

Nowadays, curating is to be found everywhere except museums. *The New York Times* defines it as 'a fashionable code word among the aesthetically minded, who seem to paste it onto any activity that involves culling and selecting. In more print-centric times, the term of art was 'edit' – as in a boutique edits its dress collections carefully. But now, among designers, disc jockeys, club promoters, bloggers and thrift-store owners, curate is code for 'I have a discerning eye and great taste.'

'It's an innocent form of self-inflation,' according to linguist John H. McWhorter. 'You're implying that there is some similarity between what you do and what someone with an advanced degree who works at a museum does.' Pretending, in other words. Going upmarket without justification.

Curvy: Fat – when clothes are being sold to this demographic.

Cut a deal: What everybody is invited to do. You can cut a deal with the guy selling the car you want to buy. Of course, it'll still cost you an arm and several legs, just as you expected, but at least you'll have the consolation of telling people you cut a deal with the garage. This is part of an advertising approach that flatters stupid, venal or plain greedy customers by casting their objective as a challenge: Can you measure up to this hamburger? Heroism through obesity.

Cyberphobia: The terror of everything online that results from having been a moron and sent all your credit card details to a total stranger posing as your bank manager.

Cynicism: The last refuge of the embittered, it allows people to be knowing but not knowledgeable, weary but not wise. Cynicism is what puts TDs in the Dáil bar, early in the day, every day, bitching and looking out for a journalist to leak them backstairs gossip. It is a slow sour poison, found, strangely, in and around politics more than any other profession, despite the fact that a career in politics means you can save lives and generally change the world for the better.

D

Day job: What you should never give up.

Dead catter: The individual who always spots what's wrong in the workplace and brings it to either their colleagues or their boss like a dead cat, never taking any responsibility for fixing the issue.

Death café: Now present in thirty-one countries, death cafés facilitate discussion about managing the last taboo: death. Death is the new life. American writer Caitlyn Dougherty made a bestseller out of *Smoke Gets in Your Eyes,* based on her experiences as a crematorium worker. A TV series is on its way.

De-baptised: New term developed to cover the removal from a handbag of the name of the woman instrumental in the design of the handbag.

Here's the back story. Jane Birkin acts and sings and travels. On one of her flights, during the 1980s, she spilled the contents of her handbag in the aisle of the plane.

A man who helped her retrieve them observed that she needed a fashionable tote and suggested he might be the man to produce one for her, he being the CEO of Hermès. The two of them designed what was called the Birkin bag, which is one expensive show-off piece of gear.

Then PETA, the animal rights activists, got up on their hind legs and claimed that the crocodile and alligator versions of the Birkin were based on incredibly cruel treatment of these reptiles. So Jane Birkin wrote to Hermès asking that her name be taken off the bag. They paid her €30,000 a year for it but she always, she says, gave that money to charity.

Defensive: The most maddening accusation levelled at anyone explaining or contradicting anything: 'Now you're just being defensive.'

Democracy: A governance system so virtuous that nations who have it browbeat those who don't want it, in tropical camps where one of the basics of democracy, the principle of 'innocent until proven guilty' doesn't apply.

Reminiscent of Voltaire's definition of an important profession: 'Doctors are men who prescribe medicines of which they know little, to cure diseases of which they know less, in human beings of whom they know nothing.'

Demons: The new scapegoats. Nobody's an alcoholic or drug addict any more if they're famous. They're 'battling their demons'. Poorer folk don't get demons to battle.

Déjà vu: Widely misused term which actually means having a sense that the event or experience currently happening has already been experienced, even if it hasn't.

Most irritating misuse? When someone talks of 'déjà vu all over again.'

Developmental war-gaming: Chronic condition rampant among south county Dublin mothers. Involves bragging loudly in the playground, school yard, playgroup or coffee shop about how quickly their astonishing child is hitting its developmental milestones. Leads to counter-claim by adjacent mother about the celerity with which her darling reached the same milestone.

– *Mother 1*: 'Milo can run backwards while reciting the Japanese alphabet and he's only ten months.'
– *Mother 2*: 'Oh, that's lovely. Sebastian can solve complex algebra and build robots and he's just turned nine months.'

Diagnosis: According to Dr Richard E. Cytowic, 'machines have corrupted the word diagnosis, "through knowledge", which once referred to the physician's knowledge of the fabric of the human body as well as its spirit.'* Now 'diagnosis' has come to mean a deferral to tests.

Diet: Anachronism replaced by the grammatically appalling 'eating healthy'.

Digital detox: Taking time out from the internet. Now classed by people who are hooked on it as an addiction, which elevates the problem and renders the 'addict' less culpable.

Digital cruelty: 'If you're going to be a blogger, if you're going to tweet stuff, you'd better develop a tough skin,' says John Suler, Professor of Psychology at Rider University
Suler, who specialises in what he calls 'cyberpsychology', suggests that anonymity and distance disinhibit the troll, so they communicate in cyberspace as they would never communicate face to face or in a situation where they would be known to the author.

---

* Dr Richard E. Cytowic, *The Man Who Tasted Shapes*, New York: Putnam, 2003.

'Rude language, harsh criticisms, anger, hatred, even threats,' are the result of this disinhibition.

Remember two things, should you be subject to digital cruelty. The first is that people are much more easily 'reached' and affected by the negative than by the positive. So we seek out the negative comments, imprint them on our souls like a tattoo and gloss over the positive. Best way to get them out of your mind is to do something that totally engages you, whether it's playing a concerto, knitting a jumper or ringing a pal about quite a different subject. The second point is that nobody else is paying as much attention to it as you are. They'll forget about it. You can too.

If the digital cruelty is part of a wider pattern of harassment or edges into credible threats to your life, go talk to An Garda Síochána.

Dill: Herb with long stringy tendrils which is wonderful with fish and almost everything else. Only fully appreciated in Russia, where they each eat enough every year to put shame on the rest of us.

Dirty word: Like 'cancer'. Back in the 1950s, a woman named Fanny Rosenow survived breast cancer and decided to set up a support group. So she telephoned *The New York Times* to buy an ad. Bit of a flurry at the receiving end and then the executive taking the call bit the bullet.

'I'm sorry, Ms Rosenow, but the *Times* cannot publish the word breast or the word cancer in its pages,' he told her. 'Perhaps you could say there will be a meeting about diseases of the chest wall.'

Things have changed a bit.

Dishwasher: An invention which divides every household straight down the middle, the line being drawn between those who know how to stack it and like doing so and those who hate it and fling unscraped crockery in it at random, or use it to turn Waterford glass irretrievably milky. It was designed to improve marital bliss by obviating rows about who was due to do the washing up. Instead, it replaced those rows with gender-defined screaming matches on how to stack the bloody thing and, let's be sexist here, women know best.

Disinterested: Not the same as uninterested. Uninterested means you don't care. If you are disinterested you might or might not care but not because you stand to make a profit from the deal. I might be, indeed am, uninterested in your half-marathon, but might subscribe to your charity because I am so disinterested.

Disruptive: The business that makes bits of the businesses around it in the same area. Blogs making bits of mainstream newspapers is one example. Scanned email making bits of the use of the fax is another. Commonly used to big up a business that, in fact, is pretty run-of-the-mill.

Distraction: Determination not to be one is the key reason for resigning from high office, if you were to believe the resigners, who, having been caught bonking the nanny/au pair/personal assistant, or having their hand in the till/in the drug stash, or being a tad more indebted to a gangster than is seemly, come nobly out in front of the cameras, clutching their printed statement, and announce that, in order to prevent the issue becoming a distraction, diverting attention from the wonderful work being done by the government or corporation, they're going to go home gracefully to spend more time with their families. Strangely, journalists never go to the resigner's home address and ask the family how they feel about this extra time being wished on them by someone who until recently was bonking the, etc. Chances are they don't look forward to it. But will they have a choice? Nope. Nobody can reject the arrival of a repentant sinner. Even if they're not that repentant, they get a free pass into their own home.

Douchebag: Abusive term which makes no sense in Ireland, where, for some unexplained reason, douching has never been the activity *du jour*. And let's not go any further on this theme, thank you.

Do you know who I am?: Frequently asked by the once-famous and by the nearly-famous when a) denied entry to the VIP section; b) stopped by a Garda, or; c) at the receiving end of perfectly civil advice from a call centre or banking official. Best answer? 'Yes. So?'

Doghouse: State of extreme domestic disadvantage men find themselves in, unconscious of the irony that they're usually in it because they have behaved like a sex or alcohol hound. No man ever tells another man what he has done wrong without first offering the universal qualifier, 'I'm in the doghouse.' Sympathy rather than judgement is the traditional response, largely because the other guy figures he could be next up.

Doing more with less: Unless it's the mass murder of those who use this phrase, we should give it up. Now.

Doing more with less is a tortuous way for politicians to say: 'We will spend your money more wisely and get better value for it.' Or, worse, to say: 'You will work harder for less pay because the nation's a bit short, these days, when it comes to ready cash.'

Doorstep: Unexpected encounter wherein the target is accused, as he/she gets out of their car, of crookery, marital infidelity or child abuse. The best gig in broadcast journalism or the worst nightmare, depending on which side of the microphone you find yourself. When doorstepped, ignoring the repeated questions and running is much worse than standing your ground or telling the microphone-wielder to eff off sideways.

Double-cheek kissing: Sometimes called 'air kissing'. Requires rules of the road. Once we are sure that you go to the left first, we'll get enthusiastic about it. Until then, absent a mouth guard to protect our teeth, we're leaving it alone, thanks all the same.

Drawing the line: A lost art, replaced by the licence to overkill.

Dress-down Friday: Quaint concession dating from when people wore suits to work.

Drone: Remotely controlled flying mechanical device first used to kill people in wars. Now on the way to killing people in peacetime, as passenger planes increasingly encounter them in flight. It is, grimly, a matter of time before one of these delivery systems brings down a fully-loaded passenger jet.

Dr Google: The best friend of the hypochondriac. Drives GPs and medical consultants out of their tree because patients arrive, having visited Dr Google and convinced themselves that they have the worst possible example of whatever ailment they're sure they have.

Those who consult Dr Google should remember the axiom that used to be shared with medical students who tended to opt for the most obscure and threatening diagnosis, based on presenting symptoms: 'When you hear hoofbeats, think horses before zebras.'

Dummies, dodos, pacifiers: Thumb-sucking is cheaper and simpler but is hampered by the myth that it will lead to prominent front teeth. Harper Seven, daughter of Victoria and David Beckham, has her own little place in history as the first kid globally soother-shamed. Before she even reached seven except in her name.

Dust Lady: Briefcase Man. Captured by press photographers in the direct aftermath of the collapse of the Twin Towers on 9/11. They loomed out of a landscape made cinder-snowy by burned office papers floating, lighter than air, ploughing through inch-deep ash silencing their steps. She was empty-handed, her palms held upward in a gesture of baffled terror. Backlit by a curious yellow hue, the picture had an air of infinity to it, as if the Dust Lady were one of the lava shapes in Pompeii. She seemed stamped forever with horror and despair.

The Briefcase Man, on the other hand, seemed unbothered and busy, as though this unprecedented attack was just an interruption to be coped with. As though he was demonstrably on his way back to a normality that was expecting him by a particular time.

After a couple of years had passed, journalists went back to find the Dust Lady and the Briefcase Man and found them to be living lives that might have been predicted by the photographs taken on the day of the atrocity.

The Briefcase Man was back in business and happily so, using the briefcase he had carried on the day, because no damage had been done to it, wearing the suit that had been greyed by dust, because, once it was dry-cleaned, it looked and felt fine. He was a man sustained by his own ordinariness and his capacity to fit the extra-ordinary into it and subsume it.

The Dust Lady, on the other hand, was not doing well at all. She was in the depths of depression and her journey through the slough of despond didn't look like it was going to finish any time soon. Her misery and the fear she associated with anything that happened suddenly near her was matched by her fear of any plane spotted flying overhead. This situation had been complicated by drug dependency which had, in turn, led to her losing custody of her children. She was undergoing therapy and as time went on, she was to get clean and sober but it came as no surprise to learn, in 2015, that she had died of stomach cancer. The prediction of an early – or at least relatively early – death was present even in that first mustard-shaded shot. This woman was never going to survive what had happened to her.

E

E-cigarette: A substitute allowing for tactile pleasure and pleasant posing, much loathed by one-time Minister for Health James Reilly as a gateway to real smoking. Recent research suggests that he may be wrong. Or not totally right. But don't knock him, anyway. He has fought the good fight against Big Tobacco.

E-commerce: Means whereby tat and other unwanted goods or services are sold to the gullible. We Irish have mastered it, hence the proliferation of the headquarters of internet giants in Dublin. Well, there's also the tax thing. Oh and we are the most educated, bright, committed workers in the world. Of course.

E-voting: A great idea that met with the overwhelming approval of those involved in the pilot from the voting side of things. From the politicians' side of things, not so much. The sudden brutality of one well-known politician learning about her destruction without going through the phases of accommodation provided by counts and recounts was shocking to watch and probably immeasurably more shocking to experience. Then the nerds got at the idea and it went and died. Expensively.

Echo chamber: An echo chamber is a greenhouse dedicated to the propagation of groupthink. To be found in media and in workplaces. In workplaces, a small group of managers who talk to each other may get a completely wrong view of what the rest of the employees or the customers feel on any issue.

Economists: The new rock stars. Main difference is that economists don't wreck hotel rooms. Give them time, though.

Economic migrant: This is the man or woman – and their children – whose fabulous humanity is reduced and diminished thus. They have no story, hopes, dreams, names, allergies, intolerances, grief, spectrums. Handily enough, they all seem to be black or brown. Tanned anyhow. Unlike Auntie Bridie – blue white – who went to New York that time on the liner and gave us the nine million cousins, half of whom brought 'civilisation' to I-raq. Yeah…

Economy, Stupid: Given ridiculous credit for putting Bill Clinton into power, a hand-lettered sign that adviser James Carville stuck up on the wall of the war room in election headquarters. Remembered as reading 'It's the economy, stupid.' The whole sign actually went like this:

– Change vs. more of the same
– The economy, stupid
– Don't forget healthcare

Ecumenical: Replaced the term 'mixed marriage'. Associated with one of the best Father Ted episodes, ruined by idiots constantly referring to 'an ecumenical matter'.

Elderly primagravida: Used to apply to women pregnant for the first time in their thirties. Now, courtesy of science, applies to women who are much older – like Marks & Spencer executive Laura Wade-Gery, who is fifty, married to a sixty-seven-year-old.

Election: One is held every few years to see how inaccurate the opinion polls are.

Electronic shut-in: Someone who rarely leaves their home, or even their bedroom, because they can access all they want electronically and devote their time, instead of dealing with challenges like real live people and fresh air and weather, to bitching and moaning *about* people who live in the real world and do real things.

Foreseen more than a hundred years ago by E.M. Forster, in his short story 'The Machine Stops', where a woman named Vashanti lives in electronic autonomy: 'Then she generated the light and the sight of her room, flooded with radiance and studded with electric buttons, revived her. There were buttons and switches everywhere – buttons to call for food for music, for clothing. There was the hot-bath button, by pressure of which a basin of (imitation) marble rose out of the floor, filled to the brim with a warm deodorized liquid. There was the cold-bath button. There was the button that produced literature and there were of course the buttons by which she communicated with her friends. The room, though it contained nothing, was in touch with all that she cared for in the world.'

Em: Verbal filler used by speakers who haven't worked out how to be interesting, understandable and memorable. Disappears in the presence of content.

Embarrassed: The emotion experienced when shame would be more appropriate. As in the shoplifter who nicked expensive cosmetics, was nabbed doing so and convicted for it. Her lawyer described her in court as 'very embarrassed,' instead of 'deeply ashamed'.

Empathy: Supposed to mean metaphorically standing in the shoes of the suffering but, in fact, fast becoming a toe-crushing invasion. Empathy is the hanging of teddies on trees for murdered children we never knew – or perhaps should have made it our business to know.

Empathy is used to plough past boundaries into the agonised and agonising personal space of strangers with cards and garage flowers.

Epiphany: What Virginia Woolf called 'a moment of being' when a sudden flood of light illuminates a life.

Er: Verbal filler that appears in print versions of communications. Never happens in real life.

Erotic capital: What women should use to get ahead, according to a professor of sociology at the London School of Economics, Catherine Hakim. Hakim's book, *Erotic Capital: The Power of Attraction in the Boardroom and the Bedroom* says beauty, sex appeal, charm, dress sense, liveliness and fitness should be used by women to help their career progress. She maintains that good-looking lawyers earn between 10 and 12 per cent more than average-looking colleagues.

Even (as in 'What does this even mean?'): The use of 'even' can be sharp and pointed, as in a story told by Today FM's Dermot and Dave, wherein one of them was noticed by a passing couple, the male of which reminded the female, in an undertone, that 'Yer man used to be on *The Republic of Telly*,' to which came the contemptuous response: 'What does he even do now?' Mostly, it is neither sharp nor pointed and should be eschewed.

Everything happens for a reason: No, it doesn't. This is just pointless self-soothing and ignores the random, which is what rules all our lives.

Excuses: Dog ate homework has longevity but some of the newer ones are unique. Like the AirCoach driver steering the vehicle on the M1 using his elbows in order to free his hands to swipe across the screen of his iPad. He said that because it wasn't a smartphone, he didn't think it would be a problem.

Excuse letter: The best was created more than a century ago by the short-story writer O. Henry:

'Dear Bill,

　'Fact is – er – that is to say – er – er – you know – I – er -er, well, I was – er – er – I mean – the – er – er – you know.

　'Hoping the explanation is entirely satisfactory, I remain as ever thine.'

Experience: What every tourism resort now offers. Because nobody can drum up their own natural experiences.

Eyewitness: One who, in a court case, is immeasurably inferior to circumstantial evidence. Studies show that more than half of those wrongfully convicted of crimes in the US were convicted on the basis of inaccurate eyewitness testimony.

Eyes: Difficult in fiction, where it is easy to encounter sentences like: 'She fixed her eyes reproachfully on him and his fell to the floor.' Sometimes, the eyes of a character fall into their coffee cup. It's disturbing for the reader and bad for the character's contact lenses.

F

Fab: Term used by 'the girls' (see page 88) to describe any photo of one of the girls posted by herself on social media. Used without irony.

Facebook: Our own little media outlet on which to tell the world what is happening in a life, boast about holidays, new cars, engagements, babies, weddings and meeting celebrities – and post the pictures to prove it. Hooks its users by initial reinforcement and subsequent agony, like alcohol, Solpadeine and crack: the more 'likes' you get on a status, the more special and popular you feel. The more you are attacked or, worse still, ignored, the more depressed you get, with some experiencing withdrawal symptoms because they haven't got the latest update.

Once you post a status, it's there for life (even if you delete it). Facebook is like having your own public toilet door, except that it lasts forever.

'I'd put getting off Facebook ahead of addressing the Eighth Amendment in terms of importance. I was comparing the whole of my life to the best of other people's lives and everybody owned a little part of me. When I came off it, I would meet people who would accusingly say, "Where've you been? I don't know what you're up to? which actually meant "I hate not being able to keep tabs on you.'" Stefanie Preissner, actor.

Faceplant: To fall on, or faint, face downward, or to make an error comparable to such a physical collapse. Wrongly attributed to the unfortunate from BMW who collapsed while making a speech in September 2015 and had his faint go viral. It is incorrect to describe what he did as faceplanting, because – oddly – he fell backwards. (Who faints in that direction?) Gave the back of his head an awful whack but showed that even the soles of his shoes were as impeccably clean as if he had planned to show them to the world.

Facetime: What it sounds like: the crucial face-to-face time vouch-safed by a star, a minister or a client to their servitors. The one with the most facetime wins. The one with the diminishing facetime needs to start hawking their CV around.

Fad: An archaic term no longer used. Once used to describe expensive passing fancies like bulletproof coffee and food intoler-ance tests. (See page 81.)

Fail: Has been added to the nouns indicative of disaster, error, mis-judgement or ugliness, having lurked over among the verbs quite happily for centuries. It is now possible to have a hair fail, a career fail, a selfie fail, a concert fail or a love fail. However, in the interests of precision, should your boob escape your clothing in the middle of a televised event, that is not a dress fail. It is a wardrobe malfunction.

False teeth: Dangerous and ugly contraptions that, mercifully, are dying out. George Washington had them. His version had a spring at each side on the back, to prevent the mortifying possibility of the top set falling out.

The spring was so strong that he had to keep his mouth clamped closed all the time, which gave him the excessively grim appearance he has on the dollar bill.

False teeth – the favourite topic of Blackpool postcards designed to be funny – became so popular when dentistry was an agonising process that a common wedding present to young bridegrooms, and sometimes to brides, was to pay for all their teeth to be removed under full anaesthesia to prevent future misery.

Problem. The bones of the human jaw require to be worked. Unworked, they shrink, which means that the false teeth fit less well with every passing year. This leads to the application of smudgy adhesive to the dentures, which doesn't work, and to major dietary changes. In other words, the wearers end up eating nothing but mashed potato and white bread.

Professor David Harris, author of *The Dental Amputee,* maintains that false teeth measurably shorten the life of those who end up wearing them.

For these and other reasons, dental implants are the way to go. Just have them done in Ireland, OK? Dental tourism can have disastrous consequences.

Failure: Oh, the shame of it. Oh, the defeat of it. Oh, the necessity of it, at least according to Jessica Lahey, who maintains that parents are so protective these days, their kids never get a chance to fail and get over it, which means they arrive at third level without the ability to negotiate. It all comes, according to Lahey, from the self-esteem movement of the 1960s: 'Basically, we felt that if we told our kids they were wonderful enough, then we could create this force-field of wonderfulness that would somehow repel the laser-blasts of mean comments throughout life,' she maintains. 'In some ways we're still stuck in that era.'*

---

*   Jessica Lahey, *The Gift of Failure,* London: Short Books, 2015.

Fair play: What in theory, we're all for, especially in one of our periodic outbursts of other-directed morality. As long as someone with more power, money or connections is being screwed over, we're all for fair play in Ireland. If *we* are getting screwed over, the default begrudger position kicks in.

Fair play to you: A peculiarly Irish compliment. Doesn't imply agreement with what you are promoting, just grudging and amused appreciation of the vehemence with which you prosecute your case.

Fake focus: What one might muster during the forty seconds during which the waiter lists off the restaurant's daily specials: 'We have cured yellow-fin tuna on a bed of organic micro-greens with wasabi vinaigrette.' Fake focus demands raised eyebrows, half-smiles and chin-rubbing to cover the mild panic as waiter launches into a description of artisanal cocktails.

Fame: Craved by everybody. Live by it. Die by it.

Fantasy cabinet: A media obsession in the six months prior to a general election, when one broadcaster after another asks politicians of many parties and of none who they'd be prepared to enter government with or serve in government under. Hypotheticals breeding like rabbits.

Fashion: The only way to beat it is by operating on the assumption that the toga will eventually stage a comeback.

Fashion blogging: A career option which requires neither education nor training and reads that way.

Fat-shaming: Asking aloud, 'Who ate all the pies?' Or accosting a total stranger (always female) to say, 'You have really beautiful eyes. Don't you think you should lose weight?'

The success rate of fat-shaming as a method of inducing behaviour change is unmeasured but doubtful: anecdotal evidence from those shamed suggesting it leads to increased comfort eating.

Favour: To get one, you must first give one.

Fear of flying: Since the beginning of passenger flight, aerophobia has been prevalent, as have methods to cope with it. Comedian P. J. Gallagher, for example, had such a fear of flying that he studied for and earned himself a private pilot's licence. Also the title of a novel by Erica Jong which, in its day, was shocking, scandalous and filthy.

Feedback: What managers are lousy at giving their employees. The manager believes, after a feedback session, that the employee understands they have been phoning in their performance and are one notch short of a written warning. The employee believes, after a feedback session, that the employee is stellar and should expect a bonus.

This tends to end in tears. At best. At worst, a constructive dismissal case lurks.

Feisty: Term used for female media survivors of advanced age. After a certain point, female commentators receive invitations to contribute to radio and TV programmes only if they make like Lady Macbeth crossed with Germaine Greer. Examples would be invidious.

Feminazi: Coined in the 1990s by Rush Limbaugh (the American shock jock) to mean 'a feminist to whom the most important thing in life is ensuring that as many abortions as possible occur'. Now used by men to describe any opinionated, authoritative woman who won't tolerate being patronised. When a British barrister (female) posted a screen shot of a LinkedIn communication from a senior lawyer describing a picture of her as 'stunning', some aspects of mainstream media went to work with a will, digging up stuff about her grandparents in order to shame her and – in that context – describing her as a feminazi. Also applied to women academics who objected to an eminent (male) professor saying that women shouldn't really become scientists because they distracted male scientists from the task in hand.

Fiction: Lies told for money.

Finger point: Habit of Hillary Clinton someone should excise from her physical lexicon. It's when she's on a platform acknowledging the orgasmic applause of the middle-aged inhabitants of Hillaryland and points to nobody in the crowd, winking and beaming as if she had spotted an old friend. Not on. Not credible. Not endearing.

Fire up the crazies: What John McCain said was Donald Trump's greatest skill. Which he shares with politicians, worldwide, who interpret trending on Twitter as second only to winning the Nobel Peace Prize when it comes to personal validation.

Firm but fair: Self-description of all bullying bastards. Favourite of Robert Maxwell, the definitive example.

Fist pump: Has taken over from the high five as a way to congratulate someone, especially on social media. It even has its own super-cute emoji. If you were to give someone a physical fist pump, you would lightly bounce your clenched fist off theirs. But no one really does that. It is, however, pretty hip to virtually fist-pump someone by sending a message like 'You got 670 points in your Leaving Cert. Fist pump.'

First love: For women, usually a mucky horror. For men, a thrilling first experience of intimacy subsequently idealised. Research carried out by the University of Lancaster, led by the improbably-named Professor Gary Cooper, has found that men are much more likely than women to carry a torch for their first love: 'It tends to be a powerful experience,' says Cooper, 'and the memory sticks with us as a reminder of more carefree, uninhibited days...people, particularly men, who pine after their first love are probably doing so because they're unhappy about something in their current relationship but are afraid to confront it. It is escapism and avoidance and it's not healthy.' (Someone should have told this to Dante, who carried a lifelong torch for a girl he met when he was nine and she was eight.)

Fit for purpose: You're not fit for purpose, I'm not fit for purpose, the world's not fit for purpose. This cliché of the decade is dead handy because, although it means nothing more than someone spotting a few flaws in an individual, policy, approach or institution, it's unanswerable. It's the corporate equivalent of accusing an individual of being defensive.

Floater: Those maddening black blobs in your vision when you look at a white surface.

Flu: May become a thing of the past, if new vaccines work out. They go for the stem of a molecule on the virus, the bit that doesn't mutate, and have been successfully tested on monkeys and mice.

Fondue: A culinary throwback, useful for mocking earlier generations who bought expensive gadgets that sat above a night light, allowing for the melting of chocolate or cheese contents and the dipping into said melt of croutons, chopped vegetables or bits of stale sponge cake. These days, it's important to buy pasta makers, ice-cream makers and vegetable dehydrators.

Food intolerance tests: An expensive fad aimed at hypochondriacs and designed to establish that what supposedly ails them is caused by undigested something or other. Anybody with spare cash would be well advised to buy equity in one of the testing companies, because their market grows exponentially. Or, as Barnum would have put it, 'There's one born every minute.'

Foodie: An individual who, offered the following nonsense quote, immediately knows who said it. 'In the sense that we cook food and it's served to people, we're a restaurant. But that's not much, is it? The fact is that [our restaurant] is about storytelling. I wanted to think about the whole approach of what we do in those terms.' Yep. Heston Blumenthal of the Fat Duck.

Fork droppers: Things never to be said at suburban dinner parties. Like 'We're renting', although this was a fork dropper only during boom years. Or 'I'm a banker/politician.' Or 'Would you want your son to marry another man, really?'

These are all fork droppers. They go against the zeitgeist. They lead to uncomfortable silences and straight to 'Coffee, anyone?'

Foxing: Nicking things. Blagging your way into places where you shouldn't be. All in a lighthearted way.

Fracas: Euphemism indicating punching an Irishman while calling him a series of seriously abusive terms. This euphemism uniquely applies to Jeremy Clarkson, who presented the BBC with a moral challenge in 2015.

Either they could keep him making a fortune for them or fulfill their duty of care to their workers, like the guy he punched. They took the moral choice. After an interval so long as to leach the good out of it.

Friend: On Facebook, an assortment of people you don't know from a hole in the ground and wouldn't choose to have a drink with, yet whose presence is weirdly reinforcing. Until they turn on you.

Friendship (when your friend is sick): Anyone who's had a bad accident or a major physical or mental illness will confirm that some friends they thought would be rocks turned out to be made of melting jelly when it came to supporting them, whereas some they'd never have considered as supportive came through, big time.

We preen, secure in the unearned certainty that in the same situation, we would be as empathic and insightful as a good friend should be to a sick pal.

One breast cancer sufferer who began to research the area, Letty Cottin Pogrebin, came upon so many examples of at best gauche and at worst crude remarks made by the well to the sick that she decided to write a book about it. (*How to be a Friend to a Friend Who's Sick,* available on Amazon.)

'I learned that illness is friendship's proving ground,' she says, 'the uncharted territory where one's actions may be the least sure-footed but also the most indelible; that illness tests old friendships, gives rise to new ones, changes the dynamics of a relationship, causes a shift in the power balance, a reversal of roles and assorted weird behaviour; that in the presence of a sick friend, fragile folks can get unhinged and Type A personalities turn manic in order to compensate for their impotence; and hale fellows can become insufferably paternalistic and shy people suddenly wax sancti-monious.'

Frock: Deadly word which establishes the user as being over fifty or even sixty. Belongs up there with 'blouse,' for which 'top' or 'shirt' should be used, and 'delft' for cups and plates.

F*** it therapy: A spa in Italy provides 'the profane way to pro-found happiness', the brainchild of a former London advertising executive name John C. Parkin. He and his wife have written bestsellers on the topic and host retreats at their centre in Urbino, Italy.

The therapy invites stressed people to let go of the unimportant things in life, enjoy the moment you're in rather than concentrate on where you'd rather be and, when things get tough, to exhale deeply and say 'F*** It.' According to Mary Coughlan, the blues singer, it works a treat and the food at the retreat is good too.

Fulsome: Oh, he gave a fulsome apology. I bet he did. Fulsome means lavish or excessive. It does not mean sincere.

Funeral: The ultimate Irish social event. Invitations are necessary for attendance at weddings. No invite is needed to attend a funeral. Politicians long ago recognised the emotional connectedness to which the bereaved are vulnerable and how disproportionately grateful they are for the presence of the politician. Of marginally – but only marginally – more importance in rural than in urban Ireland. Thanks to an overwhelming sense of community and curiosity in rural Ireland, local people will help out at funerals, with GAA committee members turning nearby school grounds into car parks run with military precision.

G

GAA: Ireland's own provincial, home-grown and omnipresent social and cultural organisation. Every parish in Ireland has some GAA representation. It literally brings out the best in us and the worst. Talking point and lightning rod.

Game-changer: An event or person that changes history. Often without any sense that they're doing so, like Ursula Halligan, whose personal story of living in the closet as a gay person who was also a homophobe contributed immeasurably to the outcome of the Marriage Equality Referendum in 2015.

Garage flowers: Tawdry tokens of late apology and vapid sentiment.

Gate: Suffix appended to the name of a scandal in order to suggest an association, at least of scale, with the Richard Nixon Watergate scandal. In 2015, appeared at its least felicitous in 'Servergate', a reference to Hillary Clinton's somewhat careless and gay approach to email during her time as Secretary of State.

Gaunt: Tabloid caption code for 'anorectic'.

Gender disadvantage: The instinctive hobbling of women pointed up by a Harvard Business School case study publicised by Sheryl Sandberg in her bestselling 2013 book, *Lean In*.

As part of the academic exercise, students were asked to read a story of a businessperson's achievement. Half the students read a version of the story where the businessperson was male and the other half read a version where the businessperson was female. Same story. Different genders.

The students were then asked how likeable the businessperson was. They were further asked if they'd like to have the business-person as a boss or as a colleague.

The students found the man likeable. They didn't like the woman, whom they saw as selfish.

It wasn't a case of the students who didn't like the business-woman being male in the main. It didn't matter whether they were male or female; the majority of the students came to similar points of view.

Sandberg points out that we expect successful men to be likeable but we don't expect successful women to be likeable. Which is putting it mildly.

Most successful women are assumed to be hard as nails, living bitches who are out for themselves and who hate other women.

Gendered language: We refer you to Barbra Streisand's definitions.

- A man is commanding, a woman is demanding.
- A man is forceful, a woman is pushy.
- A man is uncompromising a woman is a ball-breaker.
- A man is a perfectionist, a woman is a pain in the ass.
- He's assertive, he's aggressive.
- He strategises, she manipulates.
- He's committed, she's obsessed.
- He's persevering, she's relentless.
- He sticks to his guns, she's stubborn.

- If a man wants to get it right, he's looked up to and respected.
- If a women wants to get it right, she's difficult and impossible.

A less prejudicial example is that a man passes out or collapses but a woman faints. With the exception of the unfortunate from BMW who was described, globally, as 'fainting' when he did it between two cars at a public event when he was the key speaker. (See page 76.)

Geography: A major challenge to young Americans, who aren't that sure where any European country is or what its capital is.

Champion of a generation of the geographically-illiterate is Britney Spears. 'The cool thing about being famous,' she has opined, 'is travelling. I have always wanted to travel across seas, like to Canada and stuff.'

Ghost estate: A bleak leftover from the recession, found more in Ireland than in any other country. Developers got started on building new estates and ran out of money. Or they got started on the build and went bankrupt, leaving some estates bereft, unserviced deathtraps to the unwary and others inhabited only by one or two families who were left with the feeling that they lived on the far side of the moon.

Ghost forest: Geographical artefact, subsequent to Hurricane Katrina in New Orleans, where encroaching salt water, part of the dreaded storm surge, inundated forested land, killing trees that stand now in skeletal protest.

Ghost writing: The best fun in the world. The writer gets to meet fascinating people, interrogate them, write about them and get paid for it.

Ghosting: On the dating front, is a unique version of power without responsibility. It takes the form of someone you've been dating simply disappearing, without even the courtesy of a text to say, 'It's not you, it's me,' or, more bluntly, 'It's over.'

Reduces the abandoned one to humiliated pulp and makes the Daniel Day Lewis dumping-by-fax seem quaintly sweet.

Gig economy: Also known as freelance hell. Endless keyboard and consultancy warriors waging war against each other for sporadic fees, which in turn allows them to reflect with contempt on their parents' obsession with being 'permanent and pensionable'. Gigging used to be the province of musicians. Now it's for everybody.

Which makes it difficult to be sick.

Or get a mortgage.

According to Hillary Clinton: 'This on-demand, or so-called gig economy is creating exciting economies and unleashing innovation.

'But it is also raising hard questions about workplace protections and what a good job will look like in the future.' (For the idiotic use of 'look like' see page 116.)

Girls, the: A collective noun used by female friends of a mature age to describe themselves, in the belief that it conveys a sense of mischief and raciness.

Giving birth: Performance art requiring the presence of a cast of thousands, at least three of whom are handy at filming using their iPhone, so the event can be shared with the world. This is causing an odd outcome for the mothers, who report that they are reluctant to take medication for fear of later shaming. It is also generating a new profession: birthing photographer.

Glamping: Glamorous camping. Camping is supposed to be about the great outdoors, about being threatened by large predators and small insects and making fire by rubbing two sticks together. Glamping is for weenies. Of whom the market is saturated, which explains why places like Cavan are earning big bucks from it.

Glassing: Improvised viciousness with ghastly permanent effects.

Gluten: Up to a third of Americans now eschew gluten, the bit within wheat that holds baked goods together. We suspect roughly the same number of Irish people head for the 'Free from' section in their supermarket, and believe themselves to be healthier, brighter and generally more acceptable as a result. This belief is unsupported by medical evidence. Driven by the unqualified (such as Gwyneth Paltrow) and irritating the hell out of the sick (coeliacs, who suffer desperately if they ingest as much as a crumb of the stuff) it has been called the cool new eating disorder.

God: Of immense importance at the beginning and end of an Irish person's natural life. Belief in between these points is acknowledged but usually optional. Those calling themselves Christian tend to be characterised by unchristian behaviour.

Gotcha journalism: Much misunderstood term, mainly misunderstood by broadcasters, who believe that bellowing the same question several times at an interviewee: a) turns the interviewer into Jeremy Paxman, which it doesn't and for which they should be truly grateful; and b) proves the interviewee guilty, which it doesn't either.

All it does is scratch texters where they itch, which in turn convinces the broadcaster they have hit the mother lode of public concern.

Grace Archer effect: A complete accident getting retrospectively dressed up as a cunning plan. When ITV was about to launch, sixty years ago, in Britain, the BBC killed off one of the best-loved characters – Grace Archer – in its long-running agri-soap, *The*

Archers. The killing of Grace in a barn fire went down in radio history as a mighty stroke, because twenty million listeners tuned in and the Beeb's telephone exchange was jammed for forty-eight hours. Aha, went the conspiracy theorists, the killing of Grace was the BBC trying to take the shine off the launch of a competitor. And, it must be said, succeeding.

Not so, says the actress involved. Now ninety, Ysanne Churchman, who played Grace, says the conspiracy theory is upside down. What happened is that the Beeb wanted to get rid of her amid rumours that she was difficult to handle and thought that her character's departure would get swamped – in the public arena – by all the attention devoted to the ITV launch. They were shocked and unable to cope when it went the other way.

The Grace Archer effect applies outside showbiz, particularly in politics and in business. Advisers enter their grey-haired years living off a legend of a cunning plan they dreamed up, whereas in fact they were favoured by chaotic fortune.

Granular: A form of obfuscation engaged in by high-level inarticulates who want to sound articulate. A dead giveaway.

Gravy: A sauce the use of which would now constitute a major social gaffe, which allows the word to be used in a different way, to convey great, very good, good or OK. 'It's gravy, man.'

Grief: Is when you walk around feeling like your guts and organs are outside your body and are being savaged by raccoons on meth the size of Malta. Yes, both the animals and the narcotic. You are going stark raving mad from the pain of losing a wife, husband, child, partner, friend.

These days, instead of allowing us feel our grief – a perfectly normal response to the perfectly annihilating – wey hey, they give us pills for it.

Guru: Salesmanship used by broadcasters introducing someone who knows a little about a topic.

H

Handwriting: Also known as 'cursive'. Also known as a dying art or craft or method of communication. In July 2015, Finland decided to stop teaching Finnish children joined-up handwriting in order to free up their time to concentrate on developing digital skills, whatever they are. Only a third of American teachers are still teaching cursive handwriting. For most people, whose handwriting was always a calligraphic car crash, this is good news, although writer Simon Jenkins feels bereaved by this trend, seeing handwriting as each individual's private hieroglyph:

'Handwritten text is an expression of meaning,' he says. 'A love letter conveys its message in its calligraphy, declaring itself in curls and swoops, in size and tilt, in long pauses and fast scribbles…any communication confined to printed fonts loses a wealth of significance in translation.'

Happiness: An achievable paradox: most people can find it if they don't go looking for it. The secret to happiness is to behave as if you're already happy. People react to what they see as your happiness and reflect it back to you, whereas if you arrive with a face like a wet weekend, you lower the emotional temperature in the room by twenty degrees, making everybody else as miserable as you are. Not hanging around with toxic people helps, too, as does not checking too often on how happy you are. General happiness gets lifted to a whole new level by a good book and a packet of chocolate biscuits.

Also the marvellous moment at the end of a social evening when a woman divests herself of her Spanx.

Happy in their own skin: Meaningless claim indicating that someone has reached a self-esteem equilibrium. Said with enormous confidence. Begs the question, who the hell else's skin would you be in, unless you're studying to be Ed Gein, murderer, necrophiliac and taxidermist.

Hashtag: Frequently used in a spoken sentence, never with merit.

Hasn't gone away, you know: But dear God we wish it had. If only to kill off this wilted smartarsery.

Height: Always a lie, told in the interest of being more successful, based on the accurate belief that being taller, particularly if you are male, will give you a big advantage with potential partners and employers.

Helpless parents: Helpless parents can now pay experts to elevate their incapacity to say 'no' into a national syndrome.

Parents convinced their toddlers will hate them if they remove their soother/doody can consult child behaviour experts on how to undertake this significant challenge. This has contributed to a situation where public parks now have 'fairy trees' with 'fairy doors' and surrendered soothers swinging in a breeze filled with lies, one of which is that the fairies will give the swinging soothers to poor children, which presupposes that hygiene doesn't matter to poor children. Helpless parents, when they have a baby, regard the possibility of said baby weeping as a personal indictment. They therefore represent a substantial market for products like Calpol.

Hipster: Hipsters are going out of fashion and being replaced by Yuccies. (See page 203.)

HIQA: A body paid by the state to find other state bodies guilty of failing to meet standards they could meet if the state gave them enough money in the first place.

Holistic: When applied to health means noticing that someone's head is missing when you're dealing with their ingrown toe nails. When applied to therapy means the therapist is incompetent not in one but in several disciplines.

Holocaust: The Holocaust or Shoah stands in grim uniqueness as an unparalleled atrocity visited upon Jews, gypsies, gay people and others. It should never be used as a comparator, as businessman Johnny Ronan hopefully learned when, in attacking NAMA, he quoted the German sign that greeted those entering concentration camps, which – falsely – told them 'Work will set you free.' The crass disproportionality represented by the comparison was patent, but it took him at least two days to produce a retraction and a deeply unsatisfactory apology.

Holy Joe: Anyone who's not an atheist.

Homogenised: A variant on 'politically correct' employed by lads who have never got over the good old days when you could drink the barrel dry while propositioning whatever woman was handy at the time. Best articulated by that unmatched actor, Sir John Hurt, who says life was much more fun when he hung around with hell-raisers like Peter O'Toole and Oliver Reed.

These days, he told the *Radio Times*, 'People don't give into temptation and everything is controlled. Society is so much more homogenised and we're all expected to conform. People are censorious but the pendulum will swing back, as it always does.

'There were difficulties in those days, obviously, but life was more fun.

'We've become obsessed with the dangers of alcohol – you get newspaper articles that are entirely over the top. There's political correctness as well. I wonder who instigated that. Where does it come from and who says what is or is not politically correct? And as for the way you have to treat women these days...'

Desperate, it is. This respect thing is so dangerous and joyless. And if you're too young to remember those exciting days, read the biography of Oliver Reed to see how a genius marinaded in alcohol becomes a hopeless case who screws up the lives of everybody around them.

Horse racing: Great excuse for dressing up if you're a woman, losing money if you're a man.

How are you? Correct answer? 'Couldn't be better.' Or 'Mighty.' Sharing the detailed extent of what has recently ailed you is a social mistake. It's a greeting, remember. Not a health check.

How did you feel? Broadcaster question which is a gloss on 'Please cry for me, right now, on the air.'

Hybristophilia: The capacity to fall for dangerous convicts.

I always say: Phrase suggesting you believe what you always say is always interesting to the rest of us. Fact is that by being so self-referential you ensure that it isn't. Who appointed you to be Stephen Fry or Mark Twain, anyway?

I'm always asked that question: Celeb answer that should never be given, because, even if the interviewer is an unimaginative slave to convention, it's pointlessly insulting to tell them so.

I'm the kind of person who: Introductory phrase establishing the user as a boring self-absorbed pain in the arse.

I'm thinking about it: Code used, coming up to a general election, for 'I'm not voting for you.'

I'm with stupid: T-shirt slogan with an arrow pointing to the side, thereby allowing funny photographs of two pals to be taken. Has now become a slogan bereft of context. Handy, though.

Ice bucket challenge: An interesting and dangerous example of international peer pressure masquerading as charity. It traces its sodden roots back to 'polar bear plunges', when people willingly and in public turfed themselves into icy water. In Boston, the polar bear plunge has been happening annually for more than a century. Credit for updating this to an internet frenzy involving buckets is claimed by several groups, each maintaining that an athlete with ALS, also known as motor neurone or Lou Gehrig's disease, was the inspiration. Confusion arises as to which athlete actually set the thing going.

Confusion also reigns when it comes to the widely-held notion that the ice bucket challenge was lethal for several of those who undertook it. The death of a young woman named Nancy Oley was widely reported, together with photographs of her experience. Except that the photographs showed quite a different girl who survived the challenge, although she says she didn't enjoy it, and nobody of the Oley name has been reliably identified as dying in real life, so to speak.

One Kentucky firefighter did die, however, several weeks after participating in an ALS ice bucket challenge.

Four firefighters sprayed water on a group of college students and, while they were at it, managed to connect with electricity from a power line. All four were shocked and one of them succumbed to burn-related injuries some time later.

For the most part, the ice bucket challenge served celebs short of a bit of personal publicity, earned some money for charity, demonstrated the cowardice of those challenged, only a few of whom had the wit to ignore the ridiculous invitation, and quickly bored the ass off the rest of us.

Iconic: Anyone whose face and name the caption writer can simultaneously remember.

Identify as: Forget what you look like, the colour of your skin or where you were born, it's what you feel like or identify as that counts. Rachel Dolezal identifies as black. Bertie identifies as a socialist.

If you break your leg, don't come running to me: classic maternal warning. Mothers in their early twenties appal themselves by parroting their own mothers. It never worked for them but internal songs demand to be sung.

I mean: No, you don't. Especially if you're a broadcaster, you don't. Good broadcaster question: 'Have you stopped beating your wife?' Bad broadcaster question: 'Have you stopped, I mean, the thing is, there's been an issue that went viral and I have to ask you, I mean, have you stopped beating your wife?'

Incident: The term the Road Safety people use to replace the old, perfectly serviceable word 'accident'.

The plain people of Ireland talk about traffic accidents. The RSA and the AA talk about incidents. This, we presume, is to make it clear that there ain't no such thing as a blameless collision. If you suggest that the pile-up that rear-ended your car leaving you a bit creaky in the neck was an accident, this implies it was random, whereas someone must be found responsible. Benefit of the doubt is so yesterday.

This, in turn, we presume, is meant to make us all consider our responsibilities, slow down and drive sober, although our guess is that the use of this neutral term just confuses the listener. It's the prospect of penalty points that make us consider our responsibilities, slow down and drive sober. Also putting our cars through the NCT. (See page 132.)

Infinity scarf: A wardrobe item which, like the cockroach, has nothing much going for it but which refuses to go and decently die. It is a continuous circle, usually of grey acrylic, wound around the neck of a woman. Cross between a bridle and an orthopaedic collar, only soft to the touch.

Inflammation: Now recognised as the common thread running through many medical conditions. Some of those conditions render the inflammation obvious, as when a sports injury happens and the tissues around the injured part become hot, swollen and painful to the touch. Not all inflammation, however, is on the surface of the body, since it can be a response to more than injury. Bacteria, viruses, toxins, alcohol, some foodstuffs and some forms of exercise can cause inflammation. Inflammation is a protective response that involves immune cells, blood vessels and molecular mediators.

The purpose of inflammation is to eliminate the initial cause of cell injury, clear out necrotic cells and tissues damaged by the original insult and the inflammatory process and initiate tissue repair.

Innovative: Unprovable assertion applied to every company by itself.

Instagram: Social media platform adopted by teenagers to escape parents and extended families on Facebook. Think selfies and inexplicable shots of food. Used to upload pictures that make your life look more exciting than it is, to gain the approval of people you don't like.

Internet of things: Everything is kind of connected. On the internet.

Internet star: Description of handy nonentity by mainstream journalist to justify basing a story on their exploits/rants.

Irk: Revived Edwardian verb meaning to irritate the shit out of. The other revived Edwardian term is 'flirt', misapplied to blunt invitations to have an opportunistic sexual freebie, seeing as we're both here.

Irony: Under constant attack from the twitterati. Witness the London Fire Brigade apologising for tweeting, tongue in official cheek, that 'no hipsters were injured' when a trendy restaurant went on fire. The fire brigade was immediately set upon by the righteous counter-tweeters, who described the initial comment as 'unprofessional' and 'not funny'. Some people thought it was very funny and couldn't see where the unprofessionalism lay. Which view may have informed the subtly conditional grovel undertaken by the London Fire Brigade: 'Sorry if we caused any offence by using the term hipsters.' In that particular case, a conditional apology was right and proper.

Is is: No. Not the Islamist terror group. A usage that goes: 'The main issue here is is that.'

Listen for it.

It ain't over till it's over: One of the quotations from baseball great Yogi Berra, who died in late 2015, having employed mangled syntax to inform some of the great quotes of all time. It was Berra who said, 'If you don't know where you're going, you might end up somewhere else,' a truth applicable in geography, business and human relations. It was he who observed, 'In theory, there's no difference between theory and practice. In practice, there is.' Berra also suggested, 'When you come to a fork in the road, take it.' And, asked about his opinions, he claimed: 'I've never said half the things I said.'

It never did me any harm: Usually articulated in defence of beating children, forcing them to eat cabbage or failing to take exercise. It is always untrue but listeners usually find it dishonestly easier to let it go unchallenged, rather than say, 'Ya think? It's not possible that it actually turned you into the twisted and thoroughly squalid bag of nasty you are today?'

Their silence reinforces the original speaker's original conviction. Sadly.

J

Jam: A word that has morphed. Used to mean sweet stuff for spreading on bread, comprising a little fruit and an enormous amount of sugar. That's now gone upmarket and is usually called 'conserve'.

The other meaning is an avocation. Whatever you're currently into. As in: 'I don't read books much any more, podcasts are more my jam.' Or: 'I don't know if this is your jam but I'm going to a Hozier concert tomorrow night if you want to come along.'

Jargon: Patois developed inside a profession or craft to exclude others: 'We good, they bad.' Jargon carries dangerous possibilities, according to Deborah Bosley, President of the international Plain Language Association InterNational (PLAIN), which believes that 'a communication is in plain language if the language, structure and design are so clear that the intended audience can easily find what they need, understand what they find and use that information.'

At a recent PLAIN conference, Ms Bosley suggested that the mortgage crisis in the US would not have happened if banks had used clearer language when dealing with their customers. And so say all of us. And it's not just banks. It's medics, the civil service, public service and commercial entities. Except those trained by The Communications Clinic.

Jest lag: When a stand-up comic isn't.

Jet skis: Invented by Satan for the use of aural and maritime polluters.

Juicing: One of the unpleasant habits of the excessively fit. They get up extra early in the morning, put unrelated vegetables, herbs and fruits into an expensive machine and bring the result to work to drink ostentatiously at lunchtime when everybody else is tucking into delightful garbage. The usual colour is cow-pat mingled with green paint.

Jumping the shark: Going way too far, stretching credulity way too much, in the hope of impressing people. Drawn from the 1970s TV series *Happy Days* where Fonz, water-skiing, jumped over a shark to impress. You'd need to be pretty desperate…

Jumpsuit: The cockroach of fashion, the jumpsuit is impossible to kill and there's always another ready to emerge. The jumpsuit makes it impossible to pee without stripping to the thigh, which is awkward and time-consuming and may get the wearer hated by everybody else in the queue. Nobody looks good in a jumpsuit. Nobody. No arguments about this, please.

Junior hurler: Failed senior hurler. Or star on the wane. More dangerous and ambitious than Machiavelli. The older, slower ones rage against the dying of the light, the referee, the crowd and the young bollix they're marking. The species has the remarkable ability to inflict physical and psychological damage on an opponent and shake their hand afterwards.

Just saying: Addition to a comment that's supposed to make it harmless or funny. Doesn't. Just saying. See?

Job creation: The incidental and unfortunate requirement to employ people in order to conduct business. Claimed as a virtue.

K

Keeping down with the Joneses: Essential behaviour during the recession. It was socially unacceptable to buy anything new, go on holidays, get a promotion or crack a smile, as misery loves company and we all needed to prove that we were in this together. When, say, in the pub with your mates, your stories of financial misfortune had to be aligned. Zero showboating tolerated.

Killjoy: The life-saving adult in the room.

Kissing babies: Habit widely and wrongly attributed to politicians. Invitations to kiss a proffered baby should always be rejected, if only because the tension induced in the kisser conveys itself to the kissee, thereby generating an emotional meltdown and a picture suggesting public child abuse. Instructively, Princess Anne, who has been president of Save the Children charity since 1970, has, throughout those forty-five years, been resolute in her refusal to engage in photographic baby-kissing.

Kitchen fails: Everybody has them. The breadmaker. The pasta maker. The bulb for separating yolk from white that you can never find when you need it and that's difficult to clean if you do find it and use it. If you haven't employed a gadget in the last two months you're never going to employ it. Give custody to someone else.

Knock: Airport. Shrine. Money spinner. (Lourdes is the same but on a greater scale with better weather.)

Knowledge: Not the same as information. We have an over-supply of the latter. Especially on subjects like obesity. Yet a majority of the public, asked about obesity, aren't clear on what causes it. Pies cause it. Among other edibles. Anything called a 'treat' causes it.

Knowledge economy: What politicians, just before the economic meltdown, told us was going to be the making of Ireland. When we were all living on cornflakes it went out of style but shows signs of reviving.

Kybosh: Or kibosh. Or, if you're Charles Dickens, 'kyebosk'. Some would claim its origin lies in Yiddish. But the true origin is in the Irish phrase '*Caip an bháis*', or death cap. May refer to the pitchcap, a form of mediaeval torture involving the filling of a leather skullcap with hot pitch before depositing it on the pate of a person the owner of the skullcap felt hostile towards. Alternatively, may refer to the black cap a judge put on his head in the days prior to announcing a verdict involving a death sentence.

L

Lackadaisical: Casual and uncaring, like the broadcasters who put an 's' in the middle of it: 'lacksadaisical'. These inserters of redundant consonants also put a 't' in 'longitude', rendering it as 'longtitude'.

Lads: A collective noun used by male friends to self-describe, carrying, they believe, the implication that they're great craic altogether.

Ladies: A value judgement dressed up as a category. They're women. Just as gentlemen are men. Full stop. Call people what they call themselves.

Langer: Cork devaluation of another Cork person. Dublin equivalent is 'complete gobshite'.

Last frontier of romance: According to Orson Welles, the west coast of Ireland: 'Unknown and unbelievable. In all Europe and the Western Hemisphere there is nothing to approach it – in this Americanised three-quarters of the globe, it is unique – the last frontier of romance.'

Later losers: Gate-crashing an event where food and drink are served. It can apply to the food and drink itself, as in 'Let's crash the launch party in the Conrad and fill up on later losers,' or serve as a post-factum departure line, as in 'Thanks for the finger food. Gotta go now. Later losers.' Occasionally used by colleagues departing a workplace holding out the promise of a subsequent encounter to those who have to stay, with an audible comma added to make it pejorative: 'Later, losers.'

Leader: Popular belief, fostered by the questions asked in opinion polls, is that the popularity of the leader is what makes or breaks a political party in a general election. In fact, it has little impact. When the Tories won the general election of 1970, the ratings of their leader Edward Heath were far below those of the party he led and when the same Tories won the 1979 election, Margaret Thatcher trailed well behind the Labour leader and outgoing prime minister, James Callaghan. The same is true in Ireland. But the myth stays.

Leadership: Nobody is a manager any more. Management is bad. Leadership, on the other hand, suggests that each member of the team is equal (check the pay packets, they're not) equally contributory (check the surly guy in the corner who never says anything at meetings because he's busy working up to be a spree killer) and equally responsible (which is why stuff doesn't get done.)

Leadership is being sold as a role in life in order to pass on the responsibility of making precise, repetitive and infinitely tedious work interesting. It isn't. It's a ghastly process for which people should be highly paid. And tightly managed.

Learned optimism: One of the most important lessons to which to attend. Professor Martin Seligman of the University of Pennsylvania did a fascinating study whereby he matched the new sales hires of an insurance company with his own. The recruits picked by the insurance company were selected on the basis of qualifications, education and experience. Seligman's team was made up of optimists, some of whom had neither a degree nor relevant experience. When the company examined the relative results at the end of the year, Seligman's optimists exceeded the sales of the other team by 21 per cent in their first year and 57 per cent in the second.

Left brain: Despised in pop psychology, it is the second half to develop, after the right brain, seat of feelings, images, physical closeness and ecstasy. Mozart had his wife read him stories while he composed. This is believed to have distracted his left brain with spoken language, allowing his music-oriented right brain to express its genius.

Legacy: What naïve politicians believe they will leave behind them. Notoriety or obscurity is what they'll actually leave behind them.

Legit. I mean.

Leggings: Thick footless tights the wearer thinks make her look slender and sexy but which make her arse look fat in this while creating an unattractive underwear look.

Leverage: Grossly overused in business-speak: 'How can we leverage that experience and apply the learning elsewhere?'

Liar: Lying is something most people do, several times a day, every day. 'We are thoroughgoing liars, even to ourselves,' says Robert Trivers, who has studied our duplicity. 'Our most prized possession – language – not only strengthens our ability to lie but greatly extends its range.

'We can lie about events distant in space and time, the details and meaning of the behaviour of others, our innermost thoughts and desires and so on. But why, why, self-deception? Why do we possess marvellous sense organs to detect information only to distort it after arrival?*

Seems pretty bleeding obvious to us. We lie about ourselves because we prefer the version we make up to the one we grew up with.

Liberal view: Believed by people who claim to have it as rooted in a philosophy of equality and freedom. Increasingly linked to the coercive and dogmatic promulgation of a singular faith.

Lickarse: Boss or superior-flatterer.

Lid: Derogatory term for uniformed police officers.

Like: Unacceptable filler inside a sentence: 'So I was like, Dad, like it's so slack that you want to like supervise me online.' Acceptable at the end of a sentence from a Corkonian: 'You need to get a small bit of a grip, like.'

LinkedIn: Social media site everyone in business is on, although the majority are not particularly sure why.

Liquidity: You can be solvent but not liquid. If, say, your sole asset was the Empire State Building or a gold filling in your teeth, you would be solvent but unable to buy a sandwich. You would be illiquid. Which is not a good thing to be. Cash is king.

Litter: The minute you mention the word 'litter', the eyes of Irish people glaze over like one of those metal shutters coming down over a shop window at closing time. It seems at one and the same time trivial, irritating and somehow inevitable and actually it's none of the three.

---

*   Robert Trivers, *The Folly of Fools*, Basic Books, 2011.

It's not an inevitability, despite our cities, particularly Dublin, generally coming badly out of surveys. Although it's important to point out that not all of the capital fared badly in a survey conducted in 2015. The north inner city, which has tended to flunk such exams, showed an improvement worthy of mention by the organisers of the Irish Business Against Litter research.

Nor is it a trivial irritation. Litter is part of the loss of a neighbourhood's self-respect, part of a wider surrender to lawlessness and community contempt. Just as failure to take care of personal hygiene speaks to a deterioration in the sense of self in humans, failure to take care of city housekeeping speaks to a deterioration in the sense of belonging, which is one of our most basic needs.

A ghastly high-rise disaster in the US city of St Louis some time back called Pruitt-Igoe, which started with hopes as high as the apartment blocks of which it consisted, gave rise to so much murder, mayhem, drug-addiction and terror that, before it was dynamited, sociologists moved in with clipboards and questionnaires to try to work out why it had become such a littered, derelict horror.

One of the simple forehead-smacking insights the Pruitt-Igoe researchers gained was that an area that belongs to everybody belongs to nobody. Think of allotments. Each is owned by someone – by one individual – for the duration, so they compost it and weed it and love it.

That's in sharp contrast to verges and stretches of green space near roundabouts and motorways, which everybody in theory and nobody in reality owns – which is why they are filled with empty drink cans, stretches of torn plastic, bottles and whatever you're throwing away yourself.

When people, whether collected together by neighbourhood or business, 'adopt' a street, a garden or a little park, littering goes down. This seems to be because everybody feels responsible and ordinary folk pick up a wrapper that's been dropped, rather than assuming it's the job of someone employed by the local authority. Seeing this happen changes the attitude of potential litterers.

In this regard, one of the great pioneers was Disneyland. From the very first, the Disney organisation trained its every staffer to notice anything out of place and take care of it, rather than ignore it and hope someone else took care of it. That, applied to litter, created a positive culture of personal responsibility, which is a bureaucratic way to express something that isn't bureaucratic at all: visitors to Disneyland and Disneyworld got the subliminal message that littering just wasn't good. So they did much less of it.

Listening: A lost art. The word means to list, to lean to one side, a stance seen today only in response to the exigent call of the mobile phone. Today, we have to pay people known as counsellors to listen to us.

Previous eras may not have been that much better, if we believe Seneca, who lived in 4BC and who wailed, 'Listen to me for a day… an hour!…a moment! Lest I expire in my terrible wilderness, my lonely silence! O God, is there no one to listen?'

Listicle: A cross between an article and a shopping list, pioneered by Buzzfeed, designed at once to pander to and promote the shortening attention span of web surfers:

- 10 world leaders who had rabies
- 5 signs your marriage is on the rocks
- 3 foods you should never eat
- 9 sets of identical twins with measles
- 5 weird tips to lose your belly
- 7 celebs you didn't know ate frogs.

Note the use of the word 'weird', a constant in listicle discourse because it appeals to people who can't be bothered with scientific evidence and prefer to go with pure craziness.

Literally: Now, stand fast and listen up. If you say you would literally die if you met Hozier, you are wrong. You might metaphorically die if you met him, although we can't see why. Most people now say 'literally' when they mean 'metaphorically'.

LOL: This acronym, which stands for Laughing Out Loud, has become a casualty of elder use. Elder abuse quite different and a more serious thing but elder use kills off fads quicker than well-directed swatting kills off bluebottles. Once parents and grand-parents cottoned on to LOL, it developed, for younger users, the subtle patina of gangrene and their rejection of it was quickly noted in a Facebook survey.

In one week in May, 2015, it reported: 'The most common laugh is haha, followed by various emoji and hehe. Age, gender and geographic location play a role in laughter type and length: young people and women prefer emoji, whereas men prefer longer hehes. People in Chicago and New York prefer emoji, while Seattle and San Francisco prefer hahas.' 51 per cent of users go for haha, 33 per cent opt for emoji and 13 per cent prefer hehe. LOL, according to this survey, had shrunk to less than 2 per cent and even lower among teens and early-twenty-somethings.

God love LOL, it was doomed from the moment the *Oxford English Dictionary* included it in its 2011 edition. That was after it had been around since 1989. But it takes time for the establishment to get around to acknowledging new usage.

It also takes the establishment time to understand it. David Cameron, for example, when leader of the opposition in the UK parliament, was revealed to have been *flúirseach* in his deployment of LOL. The only problem was that he thought it meant lots of love. Which must have made his texts confusing to their recipients.

Longitude: No, it doesn't have a T in the middle.

Look like: Pointless verbiage added to common propositions, which is to imagine an end result. 'What will hospital care look like in the 21st century?' would be a classic example. Who cares what it will look like?

Love (and hate): Both at one time used to describe intense emotion. Now applied to hot water bottles and dairy produce.

Loved-up: Icky term used to categorise couples: 'The loved-up pair of Amy Huberman and Brian O'Driscoll.'

Luggage: The cases routinely loaded on to aircraft before Ryanair arrived.

Luminous: Usually applied to prose in reviews of books written by reviewers owning an impoverished vocabulary.

M

Macarons: Repulsively sweet, coloured and gummy biscuits that have inexplicably become popular.

Mc/Mac: The prefix of many Irish as well as Scots surnames. Technically means 'son of' but only those prepared to do grammatical contortions within the Irish language ever change it for daughters.

Make-up: Face paint. Subtle, in its use, is good. Even on stage. Laurence Olivier was so hooked on elaborate make-up that his wife, actor Vivien Leigh, once said that when he played Othello his make-up arrived on stage five minutes before he did.

Marmite: All together now: 'You love Marmite or you hate it.' Most people hate it. Guinness used to do a version called GYE (Guinness Yeast Extract) that tasted marginally better but the key thing is that a century ago a young English physician named Lucy Wills travelled to Bombay to study a kind of anaemia endemic there which couldn't be reversed by any of the treatments of the time. Wills found she could cure it with Marmite, a dark, yeasty spread then popular among health fanatics. It turned out that the key component in it, that made it so effective against the Bombay anaemia, was folic acid, or folate. Which, later, was found to reduce the incidence of spina bifida in the babies of mothers who took it in advance of getting pregnant and during the early months.

Marshmallow test: 'It began in the 1960s with preschoolers at Stanford University's Bing Nursery School, in a simple study,' says psychologist Walter Mischel,* who dreamed it up. 'My students and I gave the children a choice between one reward, (for example, a marshmallow) that they could have immediately and a larger reward (two marshmallows) for which they would have to wait, alone, for up to 20 minutes.'

The children were observed and the struggles they went through to restrain themselves during the twenty minutes were funny and instructive. Some of them wisely turned their backs on the marshmallows and sang to themselves.

'What the preschoolers did as they tried to keep waiting and how they did or didn't manage to delay gratification, unexpectedly turned out to predict much about their future lives.

'The more seconds they waited at age four or five, the higher their college-admission SAT scores and the better their rated social and cognitive functioning at adolescence.'

At age 27-32, those who had waited longer during the marshmallow test in preschool had a lower body mass index and a better sense of self-worth, pursued their goals more effectively and coped more adaptively with frustration and stress. At midlife, those who could consistently wait ('high delay'), versus those who couldn't ('low delay'), were characterised by distinctively different brain scans in areas linked to addictions and obesity.

It was all about willpower. Which, according to Mischel, can be learned.

---

* Walter Mischel, *The Marshmallow Test: Understanding Self-control and How to Master It*, New York: Bantam Press, 2014.

Matchmaking: Staple of a festival in the west of Ireland and of cheap TV, starting with *Blind Date*, starring the late Cilla Black, in the 1980s. After that programme went off the air, ITV gave the world *Take Me Out* and *Take Me Out: The Gossip*. The latest renditions are *First Dates* and *The Undateables*. This programming has the unique appeal to the viewer that no matter how unattractive or gauche they may be, they're not as rejectable as those they're watching.

Medical groupie: Someone insufficiently intelligent to get into medical school who nevertheless retains an obsessive interest in every aspect of health and illness. A medical groupie loves hanging around doctors and using medical jargon: show me a collapsed lung and I'll raise you a pneumothorax.

Medical groupies ask all the right questions when a friend calls to say that they, their child or their parent is unwell: When did you first notice? What colour was it? Any fever involved? Nausea? Sleeplessness? The groupies congratulate themselves when the friend comes back and confirms that their guess as to the diagnosis turns out to be correct. They stroke their chins at that point and wonder aloud whether the treatment will be keyhole surgery or administration of a specific medicine.

They know all about anomalous responses, like when someone is prescribed a sleeping pill and ends up doing nocturnal house-cleaning. They can quote the statistics of survival for almost any ailment, post-treatment. Their best friend is Dr Google. (See page 67.)

Meetings: 90 per cent of them are a waste of time. 'Meetings are indispensable when you don't want to do anything.' J.K. Galbraith.

Memory foam: We suspect this stuff got invented by accident, like the floatiness of Ivory Soap. We believe they were trying to make proper foam and left something out, thereby achieving an undecided hybrid that deflates and repellently takes on the shape of your foot, bottom or whatever portion of your anatomy you have inflicted upon it.

Merry: How drunks euphemise their condition. More properly, in *Proverbs*, 17:22: 'A merry heart doeth good like a medicine but a broken spirit drieth up the bones.'

Message: Term beloved of bad communications consultants, who believe that sending out a message defines good PR and produces results. This belief resists contemporary and historical evidence to the contrary. A classic was what King Zog of Albania did when Mussolini's army invaded his country in 1938.

He went on radio at lunchtime on the day of the invasion to call for mass resistance to the invaders: 'I invited the whole Albanian people to stand united today, in this moment of danger, to defend the safety of the country and its independence to the last drop of blood.'

King Zog had a good message. He did what spin doctors recommend: he stayed on message. End result, however, was there none. Partly because the fascists had twenty two-thousand soldiers and the Albanians had four thousand. But mainly because most Albanians didn't have a radio and the Italians jammed the signal to those who had one.

Met Éireann: A wonderful service housed in a Godawful building which tapers to the top, which makes sense if you're building a pyramid to impress the hell out of visiting pharaohs, but in land-tight Ireland is a waste of a good footprint. The Met Office gets the best complaints in the world. Met Éireann, the Irish Meteorological Service, got 180 whinges from an unsupportive public in the last year.

'Why the hell do you always get the weather forecast so *wrong*?' one of them queried. 'Today was promised terrible wet and windy when really the sun has been shining all day (where I am anyways). The local golf club had even had a major competition scheduled for today and they had it called off during the week due to the bad weather promised – which never came?'

In fact, the Met Office mostly gets it right. Where we are, anyways.

MIA: Term borrowed from military use – Missing in Action – for application to someone who has made like a mole in the face of public scandal, self-created.

Middle age: Used to start at forty and run to fifty-five. Now starts at fifty and runs to sixty-five.

Milk siblings: Toddlers from different families breastfed by the same mother. Shock, horror.

Mindfulness: A massive industry, marketed under the guise of mental health education. The underlying theory is that if you 'live in the moment' as Oprah always recommended, you will do better in every aspect of your life than if you live in the past, paddling around in yesterday's grievances or the trauma of your own birth, or in the future, scared witless of the myriad health, career and relationship disasters that lie ahead. End of story.

Get yourself a thick rubber band, put it around your wrist and snap it hard any time you find yourself worrying about negative possibilities down the line or getting bitter and twisted about your own unfair past. That'll make you live in the moment.

However, if your bucket list (see page 36) includes major-league mindfulness, go spend your money on weekends, semesters and vacations during which someone will profit hugely by telling you the obvious in six different ways and giving you exercises to prove it's the obvious.

Migrants: Janus-faced folk, mostly from Africa, who are victims when on board rickety racketeer-operated boats in the Med being rescued by our naval heroes on the LE *Eithne* but become a different kettle of immigrant fish altogether when they want to come and live here. We'll happily ferry them to shore. As long as it's someone else's shore. Although we improved a bit in 2015.

Misquote: A habit public speakers have. They are promiscuous in their attack and fact-checking is news to them. You know 'Hoist on his own petard'? It would lead you to imagine a petard was some kind of spear, whereas in reality, it was a small bomb used for blowing up gates and walls when breaching fortifications. This is back in France in the 16th century. So, far from being a long tall sharp thing you could get hung up on, if you owned it, a petard was an upside down ice-cream cone in shape, filled with several pounds of gunpowder, with a slow fuse. If, then, you were a petard-hurler and disregarded the health and safety regulations of the day and were hoist as a result, it would mean you'd be blown sky high by your own bomb. By. Not on.

Mission critical: The MD of Business X claims that mobile technology is 'mission critical' for the operation of his business. We think he means that staying in touch with each other is good when it comes to making the product. And that he doesn't mean to sound silly.

Mob: Bunch of morons. On the streets, on the airwaves or on the internet. Hazlitt, a couple of centuries back, pointed out that it's easy to have the mob agree with you. All you have to do is agree with the mob.

Mobile phone: A redundancy. Nobody refers to the mobility of a phone unless they're a radio producer anxious to get an interviewee to a landline, because they deliver better quality. Although Skype quality is pretty hot, too.

Moderate drinker: The favourite self-description of deluded drunks.

Molecule to medicine: The costly time span between when a scientist begins to test out an interesting possibility and the moment the end result becomes available to a patient via their GP or hospital consultant. Used by the pharmaceutical industry when arguing against what they see as the too-limited period during which said medicine is protected by patent, allowing them to make a lot of money from it before generics pull the profit rug out from under them.

Mojo: 'I recovered my mojo' means 'I stopped faffing around in the self-pity club and got back to normal.'

Monetise: Make money from. Mostly used by mainstream media about the potential they see in social media but have, with remarkable consistency, failed to get to materialise.

Moral negative equity: The state you enter when you announce yourself as a political candidate. Oh, you're really one of *them*…

Mother: Irrelevant designation of someone whose birth-giving capacity has nothing to do with the story: 'Mother-of-three jailed for drug-peddling.' Closely followed, thanks to the active contribution of older people, by 'Gran jailed for drug-peddling.'

Motherhood: The hand that rocks the cradle rules the world and mothers feel their job is unappreciated and pivotal.

According to the Grant Study of Adult Development, mothers may be right in their rating of the unsung importance of their contribution.

The study was initially funded by the millionaire owner of a chain of American shops which, in the early decades of the 20th century, was a precursor to the Wal-Mart empire. The millionaire was named W.T. Grant and, in funding the research, he hoped to find clues that would help him to pick great managers for his stores. The academic who dreamed up the whole idea, on the other hand, wanted to work out ways to help the United States military pick young men with promise as potential officers.

The study, run by Harvard's Health Services Department, started in 1938. It set out to follow almost three hundred graduates of Harvard from three sequential years. That meant the cohort would all be white males. (Nobody, in the 1930s, or for a long time thereafter, was that interested in applying a microscope to the lives of women or blacks.) 'It seemed sensible at the time to study an elite sample of men,' a current professor of psychiatry at Harvard, George E. Vaillant, has pointed out. 'And that's what the Grant Study did.'[*]

They were elite in that they had already won entrance into a prestigious Ivy League university and had higher IQs than most of their age peers.

Students who agreed to be part of the cohort to be studied were initially investigated at length and in a positive way. The objective in interviewing them about their family background and then interviewing their parents on the same topic was to hear what had been good in those backgrounds, as well as what had been bad. As time went on, they were followed up through questionnaires and visits from study staff, who conducted what might be called semi-structured interviews with them, down through the decades,

* George E. Vaillant, *Triumphs of Experience: The Men of the Harvard Grant Study*, Harvard: Belknap, 2012.

to establish where they were, in terms of health, earnings, career progress, relationships and self-judgement at different points in their lives.

The study necessarily concentrated, in its early years, on preoccupations of the time, one of which was the physical build of its subjects.

It was predicated, if not assumed, that tall men with broad shoulders and slim hips (who might, in another part of the world at that time, have been described as 'Aryan'), would more naturally move into the officer class and be otherwise more successful in life than men who were ectomorphs with skinny bodies or roundy endomorphs. As time went on, however, it became clear that build was irrelevant to career progress and life management.

Another early preoccupation was with strict as opposed to easy-going toilet training, which, at the time, largely thanks to Freud, was assumed to be vitally important to the developing child and their future as an adult. In fact, as early as 1945, observation of the emerging data proved it to be 'entirely without significance for future behavior'.

Although the study failed to confirm contemporary prejudices, it did identify one factor as crucial to success (in work) and happiness. That factor? Having been surrounded by warmth and affection in childhood. It was key even to military life.

When the men studied served their country in the Second World War, whether they came back as a colonel or a private 'correl-ated more highly with a warm childhood than with social class, athleticism, or intelligence', the study found.

They got promoted, then, because they were charming, easy-going, self-assured? Not so, according to Vaillant. Nothing so soft and cuddly: 'the most independent and most stoical men in the Grant Study were the men who had come from the most loving homes; they had learned that they could put their trust in life, which gave them courage to go out and face it.'

In sharp contrast, young men from a bleak, cold, isolated childhood became sitting ducks for failure, for physical and mental illness, divorce and earlier death than the rest of the cohort.

The very length of this study also established that people, no matter how bleak their early years, are nonetheless capable of change and of growth.

One such individual, portrayed under a pseudonym in the latest of several books emanating from the study, was a chronic hypochondriac in college and had, when he served in the army, what might be charitably described as an undistinguished tour of duty. When he was thirty-five, disaster struck. He was diagnosed as having TB of the lungs. That put him in a veterans' hospital. He later confessed that he was glad when he got the diagnosis and knew he could go to bed for a year 'and get away with it'. The hypochondria fell away, he loved being cared for and when released from the hospital, he cared for others as a doctor.

Although a bleak childhood skewed the odds for men in the study, arguably the most alarming finding has emerged only in recent years, as the subjects hit their nineties, when it was found that a poor relationship with a mother was 'very significantly and very surprisingly associated with dementia'.

'Of the 115 men without a warm maternal relationship who survived until eighty, 39 (33 per cent) were suffering from dementia by age ninety.

Of the surviving men with a warm maternal relationship, only 5 (13 per cent) have become demented – a significant difference,' says Professor Vaillant.

Einstein once said something to the effect that a boy who, as a toddler, had the unequivocal adoration of his mother couldn't be downed by life. This longitudinal study confirms he was correct – right up to that boy's ninth decade.

Mother ship: RTÉ

Motivational speech: A useful device allowing the speaker to cash in on their past and the auditors to convince themselves that what the speaker is saying will make a difference to their future.

Multi-tasking: Doing two or more things at the one time badly. Like the Californian man who drove and texted himself right off a cliff.

Mum: Term given by advertisers to women who, instead of children, have 'little ones'.

Used by women in social media profiles as though taking responsibility for their own fecundity should require a round of applause.

Must have: Description in catalogues and ads for women's apparel prior to the recession.

My mother adores you: Variations on this compliment include 'My father has always been your biggest fan.' The first time it is offered, whether to a writer, businessperson or TV personality, it creases the recipient with its not-so-hidden gloss of: 'I'm way too young to even know you but I want to be polite to you.' When it repeatedly happens, it stops feeling quite so offensive. Just around the point when you have accommodated to it and are reasonably accepting of it, it morphs into: 'My granny adores you.'

My mother always used to say: With the exception of the delightful collection in Valerie Bowe's book of this title, the phrase invariably introduces a Godawful cliché. You don't often hear someone quoting their mother to the effect that Freud's failure to repudiate the hysteria/rape theory is lamentable. Nope.

When mothers are quoted, they tend to be quoted saying teeth-grindingly prissy stuff like: 'You take care of the pennies, the pounds will take care of themselves,' or, 'When you're baking, clean up as you go.'

Fathers are quoted less than mothers. Not sure what that tells us about them but in a general way, we're grateful.

Name: Napoleon's veterans adored him, not least because his memory allowed him to call any one of them by name. In fact, the emperor was smart enough to have an aide-de-camp around to give him a prompt. Just as senators in ancient Rome had a slave close to them who would mutter the name of an arriving constituent, that slave called a *nomenclator*.

Nazi comparison: It is a measure of our continuing horror at the Holocaust and wider misery caused by the Second World War that the urge to compare enemies with Nazis never seems to go away. However, it is a measure of that continuing horror that makes the comparison unacceptable and – always – counter productive. A recent example was when a conservative political candidate in Quebec was forced to apologise over a Facebook post comparing the words of an opponent named Tom Mulcair to those of Josef Goebbels, Hitler's propaganda minister and proponent of the 'Big Lie'.

Nazi gold: The city of Walbryzch and the wooded hills surrounding it have become the focus of gold hunters on the rail [sic] of a hidden railway train full of gold. South-west Poland is rumoured to be one of the places where the Nazis stashed enormous amounts of gold bullion in the last days of the Second World War.

NGOs: Concern, Trócaire, the Red Cross. Pointless derogatory way to describe inspiring organisations, colluded with by the organisations themselves, God alone knows why. Non-government Organisation. Who else is happy to be defined as a negative? Non-rapist Individuals? Non-infectious Disease Sufferers? Non-childed Married Couples?

Negative equity: What happens when the economy turns your dream home into an unsaleable nightmare.

Nerves: The symptoms of adrenalin pumping through the system of a public speaker or actor in advance of curtain up or of a worker going for a job interview: trembling hands, distorted voice, excessive sweating and a conviction that the speaker will dry up, the job interviewee will get a blank or the actor will lose their lines.

Nerves and their concomitant symptoms are important signs that a hormone that makes people feel larger than life is on its way. Nobody should seek to chemically dampen down the outward manifestations of that adrenalin rush. It's usually the precursor to a great performance. Actors maintain that the moment one of their peers is not nervous before a performance is the day they should give up theatre work because they are burned out.

Networking: The brisk exchange of business cards wrongly believed to help grow small enterprises.

'They exchanged business cards and probably some kind of networking took place and it was highly useful, though really, when women networked with one another, they knew that elsewhere, men were doing this same thing and that the men's networking would likely lead to greater amounts of money and more access."

New ethical paradigm: Garbage phrase employed to justify not adhering to the permanent set of basic ethics.

Newsreader: The newsreader is shortly to go the way of the telex and the telegram. Done. Dusted. Consigned to history as a half-remembered authority figure of the 20th century.

That's according to one of them: Brian Dobson. Dobbo is pretty certain we won't have newsreaders in twenty years' time but he figures the demise of the job could come as soon as five years from now. 'People will just find news in different ways,' he says. 'I think you just have to accept that.'

The fact that roughly half of people under thirty – right now – get the bulk of their information and news from their smartphone would tend to suggest that he's right. The idea of sitting down at six or at nine to get the news of the day will soon seem terribly dated, since most of us, even now, are absolutely up to date with the news before we balance our meal on our lap while we watch Dobbo tell us what we already know.

But there's something so reassuring about news presented by someone we see as a figure of trust. And newsreaders, for three-quarters of a century, were major figures of trust and authority, starting with the guys on the BBC like Alvar Lidell, who announced the details of the Normandy landings, told the story of the evacuation of Dunkirk and solemnly told the world when popes and kings died. The early newsreaders were all male because it was the ultimate officer class within broadcasting. They had to speak Received Standard English, have perfect dignity and have gravitas dripping from every pore. When television arrived, they wore evening dress, as if to show how seriously they took their role.

---

*   Meg Wolitzer, *The Ten-Year Nap*, New York: Riverhead Books, 2008,

For the most part, they were trusted because they were utterly detached. Non-partisan in tone and inflection, they never betrayed the remotest possibility that they might have a personal opinion on anything. Until, that is, the day when Walter Cronkite, the doyen of American anchormen, threw his weight unmistakably behind the effort to end the Vietnam war and the President of the United States, Lyndon Johnson, watching the broadcast, muttered, 'If I've lost Cronkite, I've lost middle America.'

It's only within living memory that women became news-readers. Until they broke through and people like Sharon Ni Bheoláin became family favourites, it was believed that viewers wouldn't pay attention to the news if a woman read it because they'd be too focused on her dress.

Nice: Only those with an impoverished vocabulary ever use this one except to describe a legal argument: 'A nice [subtle] point, M'Lud.' A fall-back word to tell people you're not interested in describing something or continuing the conversation. Praise so pasty, it's not worth having. Say what you mean and ditch this one.

NCT: Profitable nanny-statism forcing car owners to rectify the irrelevant before paying again to have their vehicle passed as roadworthy, which it was before the state forced them to waste several hundred of their hard-earned Euro and a couple of days of their precious time. No evidence exists to prove that the NCT has improved road safety in any measurable way.

Nollaig: The woman who insists you don't really need to buy her a separate birthday present in December.

None of the above: It used to be AFF – Anybody but Fianna Fáil. In 2015, it emerged that a sizeable proportion of the populace were 'None of the Above' voters, attracted by any candidate who did not follow the tenets of mainstream party politics. This is echoed across the world, with Americans looking seriously at Donald Trump ('he tells it like it is') and Corbynmania taking over the Labour Party in Britain. We won't even mention Greece and that headbanger on the motorbike.

No offence: A way of alerting everybody to the offensiveness of the upcoming comment.

Nordic countries: The prefects of the world. Top of the class, kiss teacher in everything social, humane and decent. Also naturally blond. You can't even hate them because they gave up invading other countries several centuries ago.

Nordic model: Catchall phrase used to describe the sort of efficient public services they supposedly have Up There. Frequently cited by politicians. Such citation often immediately followed by stringent rejection of the possibility of imposing higher taxes to fund same.

Notions: A word used to describe an action by any individual with the audacity to do something above their station or outside local social norms. Sample usage? 'So and So's after getting real notions about himself. 'Twas far from kale and brunches he was raised.'

No worries: The single most irritating response to an expression of gratitude.

Obituary: The mainstay of regional media. God's score card.

Old wives' tales: Abusive term for centuries' old knowledge and wisdom which, every now and then gets validated by scientific research. Like the study in Atlanta, Georgia, which started from local healers' claims that they could make a liquid from the leaves of the sweet chestnut tree which would, when used as a skin wash, treat skin infection and inflammation.

Emory University found the old wives were right. Better than right. The liquid was effective against the hospital superbug MRSA. It didn't kill the bacterium but in some way shut down its ability to generate the toxins that cause damage. 'It's easy to dismiss traditional remedies as old wives' tales, just because they don't attack and kill pathogens,' said Dr Cassandra Quave, who led the study.

'But there are many more ways to help cure infections and we need to focus on them in the era of drug-resistant bacteria.'

On fleek: Same as 'On point' below. Meaning perfect. So you might comment on a friend's eyebrows – that they are 'on fleek' – assuming neither you nor your friend has a life.

On point: No, not a ballerina standing on her crucified tippy-toes in satin dancing shoes. As with 'On fleek' above, it means having achieved perfection. Mostly, however, used by those who have failed to reach that point to explain their ostensibly untypical failure: 'Gawd, I am *so* not on point today. Sorry.'

One of the only: 'One of the only cafés serving paleo food.' You cannot be one of the only. Only is like 'unique'. You are the only or one of a few. The same applies to 'One of the last'. Either you are the last, or you are one of the few remaining.

Online shopping: More expensive and less fun than real shopping, plus you have to stay home for the delivery to happen. Online sales account for a fifth of non-food sales in Britain. The growth in online shopping slowed in 2015.

Opinionated: Like 'hysterical', a put-down exclusively directed at women. Witness Yeats's advice in 'A Prayer for My Daughter' when he was telling her not to get into politics:

Have I not seen the loveliest woman born
Out of the mouth of Plenty's horn,
Because of her opinionated mind
Barter that horn and every good
By quiet natures understood
For an old bellows full of angry wind?

Opinion polls: A form of slow suicide employed by newspapers which, instead of using their reporters to break stap-me-vitals stories, pay non-journalists to ask 1001 people their views on the leadership performance of politicians, then fill three pages with the results, which are regularly disproved in the subsequent election.

This has been picked up by every available media outlet. Some make telephone calls to conduct a poll, with the person called being subjected, in some cases, to an automated message inviting them to click keys on their phone to register their opinion.

The coverage moves on to the opinion poller, who explains the methodology and significance of the poll and then journalists interview each other about the implications. Politicians get their fillings rattled several times a month by such polls and, when they're on the losing side, make themselves ridiculous by describing opinion polls as 'just a snapshot in time'. Yeah? So?

Organic: Grown without artificial fertiliser or pesticide, which is good for the environment but has no provable benefit for the nutritional value of the food produced.

Out of date: The most dated church around is the Salvation Army. It caused that passionate atheist, George Bernard Shaw, to write a play about it. The key moral question in *Major Barbara* is whether the Army should take money from a distiller and an arms manufacturer.

'On that point,' GBS wrote, 'the reply of the Army itself was prompt and conclusive. As one of its officers said, they would take money from the devil himself and be only too glad to get it out of his hands and into God's. They gratefully acknowledged that publicans not only give them money but allow them to collect it in the bar, sometimes even when there is a Salvation meeting outside preaching teetotalism.'

Today, the Army is a powerful worldwide church. In every American city at Christmas, its members do bucket collections at the door of every major store, bell incessantly ringing. Its single church in Ireland is alive each week with music, frequently African music.

The Salvation Army marches to an unchanging tune, red military epaulettes on the shoulder, Bible in hand. Dated as hell. And as modern as tomorrow.

Out-dark: To compete with negative predictions when things are demonstrably good, as when economists and other commentators seek tenure on radio and television programmes by being Cassandra on steroids.

Also indulged in by journalists like Joe Klein and George Stephanopoulos:

'I come from Russian Jews,' Joe said. 'Whenever things are good, we start to hear hoofbeats – the Cossacks.'

'Yeah, I know just what you mean.'

'Don't try to out-dark me on this one, George. It's in my genes.'

'Mine, too,' I replied. 'The Turks.'

Outlet: A store or mall predicated on the mitigation of shopper guilt: if it's this cheap (which it isn't, really) it would be immoral to pass it up. Wouldn't it?

P

Pap: A verb, meaning to be snapped by paparazzi. In 2015, the Duke and Duchess of Cambridge issued a warning/plea to paparazzi to stop papping their elder son, Prince George.

Paper: A commodity computers were going to make obsolete. The belief in the forthcoming obsolescence of paper is just one of the examples going to prove that the human race is lousy at predicting the future.

If paper and paperwork had diminished, shredding companies wouldn't exist and neither would green bins.

Party political broadcast: A crazy hangover from the past, still extant in Britain and Ireland because of a residual belief that advertising is evil and would lead to the selling of politicians as if they were soap suds.

Which leaves us, nine times out of ten, with a broadcast showing the leader and other favoured candidates being fawned over in public. This kind of party political achieves nothing and costs the earth.

Passing: No, not an African-American letting on to be Caucasian, or a gay person letting on to be straight. 'Passing' is the softly-softly way we now refer to dying. When someone pops their clogs, turns their toes up, encounters the Grim Reaper, snuffs it or checks out in a final kind of way, they'll be described as having 'passed' or as 'passing away'. They died, OK? It happens. All the time, it happens. And when it happens, what's left is a body. Not 'the remains'.

Passionate: What everybody claims to be about whatever they make. We've never seen a yogurt, slice of bread or glass of whiskey improved by the claimed passion of its maker.

More to the point, when you need your toilet unclogged, it doesn't much matter to you that the plumber claims to be passionate about S-bends.

Passwords: Smart way of separating good from evil. Gave rise to the word 'shibboleth', because one warring historic group, having locked in an opposing, not to say hostile tribe on one side of a river, demanded that anybody wishing to cross the river articulate that word.

The winning side had worked out that those on the losing side had a genetic inability to pronounce the sound 'sh', rendering it as 's'. Any unfortunate who mispronounced the term died on the spot and hundreds did so in one night.

Modern passwords reverse human progress. In theory, we have machines to speed up everything we do. In practice, whether it's getting money out of a machine in the wall or turning off a screaming office alarm, we each have to remember and recall on demand dozens of passwords.

Most of them are useless, anyway, because they are the date of the owner's birth or the name of their pet and therefore easy to hack into. A good password, on the other hand, is impossible to guess. ihategoddampasswords would be perfect.

Pathology of power: One of the many diseases suffered by the Roman Curia, according to Pope Frances.

Pastafarian: When a third-level college in Dublin advertised for a chaplain, it received an application from a member of the Church of the Flying Spaghetti Monster or Pastafarianism, who went public protesting that chaplaincy posts tended to be reserved for Catholic priests.

The Flying Spaghetti Monster parody church started in 2005 as a protest against the Kansas State Board teaching 'intelligent design', an elaborate rejection of evolution, in public schools. It has since become a handy catchall 'church' for atheists wishing to curtail the influence of traditional religions in increasingly secular societies. Adherents wear colanders on their heads. When it seems appropriate.

Pavement etiquette: Early examples of this trail into present times: men were expected to walk on the outside of the pavement, nearer the road, in order to take any horse-kicked mud. Today, the key tenet is: Do not read your texts while walking, because you endanger yourself and others.

Peak beard: You know peak oil? Same deal, except in relation to facial hair. The attractiveness of men with beards is waning. True hipsters are now clean-shaven. When your local tax inspector has thick, neatly-clipped facial hair, it's clear peak beard has occurred. Next.

Pension: Part of a phrase beloved of our grandparents: permanent and pensionable. Meaning that you worked for a period and then retired on a goodly portion of the salary you were on when retirement arrived. But pensions aren't what they used to be. Bismarck, the man who invented the old age pension, picked the age of sixty-five as right for it to kick in at on the basis that most of the population back then died before they reached that age.

Persistence: 'Nothing in the world can take the place of persistence. Talent will not: nothing is more common than unrewarded talent. Education alone will not: the world is full of educated failures. Persistence alone is omnipotent.' Calvin Coolidge.

Perspex podium: A dire invention which magnifies the person standing at it. 'The inventor of the Perspex podium should be shot with balls of steel.' Anton Savage on Today FM.

Pessimism: Often believed to be inborn. However, with training and time, pessimists can turn into optimists.

Pete Tong: 'It's all gone a bit Pete Tong' is rhyming slang for 'a bit wrong'. Named after a DJ on BBC.

Petite: Used to mean small. Now, particularly in retail, means short but…spherical.

Physical trainer: What TV presenters become when their telly career wanes. Better than in the old days, when they just took to the drink.

Photo bomb: Habit of the under-employed who get in the back of photographs, unbeknownst to the people in the front of the shot, and use index fingers to put horns on them. Now expanded to include any eejit who uses his or her person to wreck someone else's picture.

Pide: Turkish pizza. The new fast food. Or at least the impending fast food, with toppings like sheep's cheese, lamb and black pepper. The base must be as tender as your earlobe. (Gave it a quick squeeze, there, didn't you?)

Piece: Meaningless verbal filler: 'We need to talk about the employment piece, now.'

Pinchpoint: Where a challenge becomes a problem. As in: 'Dublin, in terms of commercial space, is at pinchpoint.'

Pink: Colour vigorously, even coercively marketed at little girls, whose bedrooms are vomitous as a consequence.

Pip-squeak: Nobody in Ireland any more describes a small noisy person akin to a human Pomeranian as a pip-squeak, out of respect for the vertically challenged and fear of their venom. We do, however, cherish Joe Eszterhas's description of one of the returns to campaigning of a former US Presidential candidate, Ross Perot: 'He came pip-squeaking back…'

Pity: The second most important gift available to anybody, no matter how financially strapped they are. Lovely line at the end of a Peter Ustinov short story, where an old writer is advising a stellar and much younger writer who has the whole plot and characterisation elements of writing nailed. 'Just add a dash of pity,' says the older writer. 'Just add a dash of pity.' Which piece of advice applies to much more than the writing profession.

Pine marten: An unsung ecological hero. Cute little guy who is saving the red squirrel, much to the delight of environmental activist George Monbiot: 'Pine martens are predators native to Britain and most of Europe,' he wrote in the *Guardian*. 'They are members of the otter, badger and weasel family (the mustelids) that are at home both on the ground and in the trees. They are, to my eye, exceptionally beautiful. They look like sinuous chestnut cats with yellow bibs.'

They are, he notes, doing away with the grey squirrel problem in Ireland with an efficiency Britain could emulate.

You may believe squirrels are equal but that's like saying Beethoven and Mozart are the same. Just as you have to prefer Mozart, you have to prefer the red squirrel. The grey squirrel you have to regard as an invader rat with a fluffy tail. According to the folk at the Wicklow Wildlife Park: 'Grey squirrels are not native to Ireland but originally came from the forests of eastern North America. The Irish population originated from a single introduction in 1911, at Castle Forbes in Co. Longford; apparently they were introduced at a wedding party.'

What kind of a mad wedding requires the importation of grey rodents? What kind of lax supervision allows the release of these horrors into the wild so that in the intervening years, grey squirrels have colonised twenty counties in Ireland? Someone needs to go ask questions at Castle Forbes.

Now, while the grey squirrels were breeding like rabbits, you should pardon the analogy, the native red squirrel, a much prettier little animal, was being squeezed out, just as happened in the UK. At the same time, the pine marten, the animal that used to be known as *an cat crainn*, because it climbs trees and looks like a cat, wasn't doing so well either, being hunted for its fur. The 1976 Wildlife Act was the first step in many to its resurgence, although the numbers are difficult to judge because pine martens aren't that social. They come out, have sex and then part company for maybe a year until the longing comes on them again. But once the pine marten population increased, it became obvious that they were knocking hell out of the grey squirrel population.

Why, you ask yourself, were these omnivores not similarly knocking hell out of the red squirrel population? Because the red lads are smaller and lighter. So they can get right out to the end of a tree branch where the pine marten can't follow, unlike the lumpier grey squirrels. A round of applause, there, for the pine marten.

Platforms: Shoes with blocks under the front bit, adding height and unsteadiness to the wearer. Platforms happen twice a century and last way too long on each visit.

Policies: What political strategies and backroom lawyers believe motivate voters. They're wrong. Voters are motivated by bias, previous affiliation, personality, self-gain, how they perceive the candidate as doing on TV and the desire for general revenge.

Political correctness: Term used to devalue protest at verbal bigotry. Watch out for the phrase 'Political correctness gone too far.' It is commonly used by male commentators/big personalities irked when anyone objects to them insulting women/LGBT people/people with a disability/migrants in the Med or travellers in the neighbourhood.

Their feeling is that if you're already dehumanised by any one of these conditions, a little more vitriol won't hurt you and if it does, get over it.

Political leadership: Political leadership is not about giving things to people. That's patronage. Peonage. Bread and circuses. Political leadership is about leading people to deliver on their own potential.

Pop-up: A temporary series of rooftop pop-up restaurants opened (and, predictably, closed) in Dublin in the summer of 2015, described by one of those involved as 'sort of whimsical summer evening vibe…an all-senses alive kind of thing.'

Potholes: Sink holes in minor roads known to swallow pre-1995 Nissan Micras. Usually filled in with tar three weeks before local elections.

PowerPoint: An invention of Satan, avoided by all good communicators. An improvement that makes things worse. A form of electronic addiction implicated in the loss of the Challenger space ship and all the souls on board.

Pragmatic: Word favoured by Fianna Fáil in Charlie Haughey's time, signifying a disinclination to obsess over principle or policy consistency.

Pranking: Practical joking designed to make someone else miserable. Pranking is also applied to a form of licensed recklessness pioneered by George Plimpton, who called it 'participatory journalism' and became famous for competing in professional sporting events, acting in a western, performing a comedy act at Caesar's Palace in Las Vegas, playing with the New York Philharmonic Orchestra, then writing about it with some elan.

Plimpton did study and train for many months before he did something like climb into a boxing ring with a professional, unlike the 'internet stars' who have devalued the approach.

Take, for example, Faisal Shinwari, who came close to drowning when he jumped off London's Tower Bridge. The same half-wit had earlier tried punching total strangers in the street, only to find that they were better at impromptu boxing than he was, and spray-painting luxury cars without their owners' permission. In these situations, his cry of 'Chill out, man, it's only a prank' proved to be as ineffectual as his Thames swimming skills.

Pre-budget submission: A ritual dance undertaken at enormous expense by industry organisations to persuade their membership that they work hard for them.

Presently: Means shortly, in the future. It does not mean at present.

Price of fame: Is loss of privacy.

Prison: Better than the old IDA advance factory when it comes to being useful to the local economy. Dostoevsky claimed that 'the degree of civilisation in a society can be judged by entering its prisons'. Which almost nobody other than the convicted in Ireland does.

Privacy: An odd current obsession, which gives us, on the one hand, a series of regulators devoted to the protection of the nation's privacy and on the other hand, a willingness on the part of the citizens to share their most intimate details with websites like Ashley Madison and their secret banking details with anyone who sends an incoherent scam message claiming to be stranded in a foreign airport without money.

Property porn: Provision by mainstream media of the stimulus which led to the property collapse and continues, post-recession, to the orgasmic delight of potential investors.

Protesting the: We're dead against. We no longer protest against or about something, we just protest it, pure and simple, be it cuts to the health budget, free legal aid or paying for water. As if the protestation itself is what matters, not the wrong we are supposedly opposing. It sounds dead posh though. Until of course of it comes to protesting our innocence. If we 'protest' that, it surely signifies our guilt?

Psychologists: The most in-demand profession, required everywhere by people who cannot cope with the normal nasties of daily life. Like economists, they are not good at predicting the future. Albert Speer, the Nazi who survived Spandau prison after the Second World War, said that one of the reasons the Allies were good at picking targets to bomb was that they had economists and agronomists identifying the right locations.

'The British, less successfully,' said Speer, 'allowed psychologists a look-in. They were as mistaken about their forecasts on German morale as we were about the effects of the rocket attacks on London.'

Psychopath: Now frequently softened to 'sociopath'. Pro-social sociopaths make great politicians and businesspeople. The great robber barons were mostly in this category. We tend to hear about sociopaths, however, in relation to crime.

'Why do psychopaths commit crimes?' asks forensic psychologist Barbara R. Kirwin: 'Very simply, because they can. Psychopaths do what has to be done – nothing personal – swiftly, efficiently, expediently. They undergo no internal dialogue, no wrestling with conscience. Rarely do I see psychopathic personalities in the therapy room, because they don't feel they have to change. But I do see them very frequently in the lockup when I undertake a forensic evaluation of a killer. When I confront these psychopathic murders, I feel what I call "thinged". Basically, you can never connect with a psychopath. You are relegated to the status of an inanimate object to be used for a specific purpose according to the psychopath's design. You are reduced, your humanity is invalidated, you are a character in his drama. You are less than human. You become Ted Bundy's Porsche."

Public opinion: According to Sir Robert Peel: 'Public opinion is a compound of folly, weakness, prejudice, wrong feeling, right feeling, obstinacy and newspaper paragraphs.'

Pulled (as in pork, chicken or beef): Meat attacked with a crochet hook to make a virtue out of it being overcooked.

---

*   Kirwin, Barbara R., PhD., *The Mad, the Bad and the Innocent: The Criminal Mind on Trial – Tales of a Forensic Psychologist*, New York: Little, Brown, 1997.

Punters: Unfortunate term used by politicians and commentators during elections, in that it suggests that voters are gambling, rather than making an informed judgement on honourable potential public representatives.

Pursuit of new business opportunities: Rationale advanced by business celebs when they get fired.

Q

Qabab: Also spelled Kebab. Chunks of meat of uncertain provenance dressed up with ethnic connotations. Useful (Like Qubala, below) for Scrabble, because it allows the player to use Q (high score) without waiting to get a U to put after it, as is demanded by most words beginning with Q.

Qubala: Also known as Kabbala. Also known as Crap-bala. A mishmash of half-understood mystical borrowings from Juddaism. Also noisy, according to neighbours of the London Kabbalah centre, frequented by celebs like Madonna and Gwyneth Paltrow, who say they can't hear their own music when the centre starts emitting screams and shouts. All going to prove that people who don't believe in something will believe in anything.

Quinine: One of the great marketing mistakes of all time. Quinine, which for centuries was the only treatment for malaria, was exported from 17th- century Peru to Europe under the brand 'Jesuit Powder'. This at a time when the Protestant church was powerful and when even Catholics weren't that gone on the Jesuits. Anyone who suffers from nocturnal leg or foot cramping should keep a bottle of tonic water containing quinine beside their bed. Works a treat.

QWERTY (keyboard): Doesn't matter whether you use two or ten fingers, the layout of this keyboard is one of life's great joys. All children should be taught to touch type, thereby allowing them to input as quickly as thought.

Quilting: An unnecessary and pointless exercise carried out almost exclusively by women with too much time on their hands. It does, however, cost little while keeping them off the street.

Quantum, Book of: A fascinating set of guidelines employed by the Personal Injuries Assessment Board to compute the compensation see page 51) due to an individual who slips on grease in a greasy spoon restaurant, falls on a broken footpath or snaps their arm in what is now called an 'incident' involving a car and another car.

    The Book of Quantum lays down how much a broken arm, nose, ankle or worse is worth. Solicitors fight *The Book of Quantum* is if it were the Bible of a religion they hated, which is pretty much the reality.

Quick Pick: Most common form of Lotto purchase in Ireland. The Irish can't be bothered to remember numbers or stick to plans.

R

Rainbow chasers: The eyes-to-heaven term used by the realists during the 1916 rebellion about the poetic dreamers among the leadership.

Raiser-uppers: Fetching wooden blocks pioneered by cabinet maker Clyde Kershaw to serve the needs of hypochondriacs who believe they will get headaches and backaches if their PCs aren't raised a couple of millimetres above their desk.

Rational: What few of us are. Novelist Flannery O'Connor said, 'I write because I don't know what I think until I read what I say.' Communications expert Tom Savage adapted this to: 'How do I know what I think until I hear what I say?' in an effort to get people to talk out loud what they planned to say before hearing it – with dismayed surprise – live on the air.

Razor wire: We knew barbed wire, before the refugee crisis of 2015. Barbed, or 'bobbed' wire, with nasty pointed additions along its course, had been used since the late 19th century, particularly in the American West, to keep animals within a particular area and to keep predators out of that area. Razor wire is a variation of barbed wire, with blade-sharp areas designed so that when the wire is used to prevent ingress by humans, those trying will at least lose chunks of their clothing and possibly chunks of their skin in the process.

Reality television: Programmes constructed from desperately contrived circumstances from which all reality has been carefully expunged. These programmes also constructed around unstable humans prompted to behave like the headbangers they might not otherwise be in order to add tension to the proceedings.

Re-imagine: Imagine.

Recidivist: Someone who used to vote Fianna Fáil, swore to anybody who would listen, after their last government fell, that they would never do so again and who now harbours secret intentions to vote FF at the next general election. The secrecy of the franchise is good for recidivists and shy Tories.

Recession-beaters: Businesses or aspects of businesses that do better in recessions than others, ergo worth investing in for when the next recession comes around, which it surely will in about seven years. Jewellers do badly but pawnbrokers do well and, as one plastic surgeon puts it, 'In a recession, facelifts go down but fillers go up.'

Recession birth weight: According to Icelandic research, babies born in a recession are as damaged by the economic woes as if their mother had been smoking during pregnancy. Babies in their first trimester in utero when the financial crisis hit were born 120gm lighter than the average and were more likely to suffer neonatal illness.

Reference: The old idea was that a reference came from someone who knew the job applicant or had employed them in the past, thus allowing the referee to testify to the applicant's suitability for the offered post.

So litigious has the employment front now become, however, that some former/current employers have adopted a standoff position allowing them to confirm that the applicant worked for them from one date to another and offer the title of their role but make no value judgement on the individual. Good thinking, Batman.

But then, the checking on references is often so lackadaisical that it has allowed a small industry in phoney references to built up. It is now possible to buy a reference online and even buy the services of a phoney former colleague or boss prepared to testify on the phone to the applicant's general wonderfulness.

On the other hand you have people – some of them well known – prepared to give references to people they know to have shown egregious lack of judgement. Take TV historian Mary Beard, who, having been trolled on the internet by a young man who made particularly invasive and nasty personal comments about her, first outed and shamed him, then met him, accepted his apology and provided him with a reference on the basis that he had learned from his mistake.

References should be real and if you ask someone for one, you should also make it clear what you hope they will say, should the potential employer give them a follow-up phone call. If they don't feel they can deliver, get someone else.

Reform: What some younger politicians think voters care about, so they come up with methods of reforming the Whip system. This belief should be subjected to the *Liveline* test: does it get talked about in the bus on the way home from the shops? Reform, as a concept, fails that test every time.

Regulation: What we have an over-supply of in every area of Irish life, with regulators out-footstamping each other lest they be perceived as doing light-touch regulation, which is what we all loved before the banking crisis.

Remains: Denoting a dead body, this use of the word needs extinction, with its demeaning connotation of a left-over bag of skin containing bones and organs.

Renaissance man: A guy with at least two skills.

Repetition: A communications essential. Makes listeners remember what's said. Plus people love it. A child having a fairy story read to them for the nth time will note if a parent skips a line and demand it be given in full. Research shows that repeating a story increases the teller's confidence in it, too. Which is good for public speaking, bad if you're a witness in a court case who got it wrong first time around.

Resile: To step back from a position. Used by those who want to make their own stepping back from a position sound upmarket and virtuous.

Resilience: One of the two traits essential to success. The other is kindness.

'Resilience is the presence, at any given moment, of emotional maturity or emotional intelligence, characterised by self-esteem and self-confidence, the capacity to create and maintain friendships with peers…a well-founded sense of trust; a sense of purpose; a set of values and beliefs that guide responses to the world; and a feeling of having some internal locus of control.'[*]

Response: What everybody says you must make when you find yourself in media cross-hairs. Wrong.

'Only way to get the fire out is to stop feeding the flame. No matter how bad, if there's nothing new to report – nothing new to feed the flame – it dies out. People always make the mistake of

---

[*]   Moira Raynor and Mary Montague, *Resilient Children and Young People*, a discussion paper published by Deakin University.

thinking they can douse the flame with their words, that they're so smart, their explanations will work like water or something. It's always a mistake to talk to the press. Everything – even wonderfully worded denials – feeds the flames and keep it stoked.'*

Rhetorical question: Asking a question, particularly in a speech, you hope that the audience will not answer, or using the device as a lazy way, in an essay or newspaper column, to get from one point to the next: 'So why would Syrians be so eager to get out of their home country?' Or, more frequently, 'Where do we go from here?'

Rhetorical questions have been used in drama to allow characters like Captain Boyle in *Juno and the Paycock* to speculate: 'What is the stars, Joxer, what is the stars?'

Rice: Once regarded as a foodstuff, now seen as an essential technological assist. A bag of long-grain rice must be kept in every office and home against the possibility of a mobile phone being dropped in the loo. Cleaned off by the owner (who else?) the phone is then stuffed into the rice bag and left for several hours, after which, if the rice force is with you, the phone will be working again. If you are caught short, a plastic bag filled with crumbled rice-cakes will do instead of raw rice.

Ride: In America, to give someone a lift. In Ireland, to score. As in sexually. So a female trainer from The Communications Clinic, at the conclusion of a course she had delivered in the US, was warmly congratulated by one of the participants. 'Best course ever,' he told her. 'Can I give you a ride?'

Right-sizing: Canning employees to protect shareholder value.

---

*   Harlan Coben, *Darkest Fear*, London: Orion, 2002.

Right to water: What we all have. At least in countries where it falls out of the sky in bucketfuls. What we do not have is the right to treated water that's safe to drink without boiling the bejasus out of it first.

Rings of fame: A term coined by a journalist after an interview with Matt Damon. Famous people, he learned in the process of watching the star, 'tend to tell stories about people more famous than they are. Matt Damon tells stories about Tom Cruise and George Clooney…

There are rings of fame, like some kind of obverse inferno, and people inside one ring tell stories about people in another.'

Risk: Aspect of life we are bad at judging. Kids list lions and tigers at the top of their answer to 'What's dangerous outside the house?' while adults take the view that they drive way too fast to be worried about cholesterol.

Roadkill: Wildlife involved in a lethal argument with a car or truck. Most recently the star of *Newsnight* on BBC 2 when *Guardian* columnist George Monbiot skinned, marinaded, cooked and served a squirrel which had been on the losing side in such an argument. In the middle of the predictable outrage, PETA, the animal rights organisation, said he had a point when he advocated the development of roadkill cuisine. 'There are millions of squirrels, rabbits, pigeons, deer killed every year,' Monbiot pointed out. 'A lot of them are landfilled. It doesn't have to be the case. It's not very nice but meat production isn't. We have become so far removed from the realities of meat production that anything that reminds us of where it comes from and how it is processed – let alone reared – is disturbing and dissonant.'

Role model: Any celebrity the media has decided it now wants to destroy.

S

Saddo: Irish term for the hopeless case who has no life.

Salubrious: Means 'health-giving', 'wholesome' or 'pleasant'. But rarely if ever used by someone under fifty years of age. Language is more of a giveaway than wrinkles, when it comes to age. That's the bad news. The worse news is that a facelift is effective at removing some of the evidence of passing time but nobody has yet invented a language facelift.

Older people speak a different language from that of their children and grandchildren. Which may or may not matter. If you're George Hook, it clearly doesn't matter, because George has positioned himself as an irascible oul' fella and is loved on that basis. Younger listeners to his show get the drift of sentences which include words like 'salubrious' without themselves using that particular term.

For less famous people, though, using outdated language can evoke responses ranging from impatience to condemnation. When an older person talks about 'itinerants', for example, they may assume it's the correct term, since that's what it was in their time. Since then, however, the rule has taken hold that you call people by whatever they call themselves and travellers assuredly don't call themselves itinerants any more than gay people call themselves 'homosexuals'. If you decide you're not going to play by that rule and describe it as 'political correctness', that, too, defines you as elderly, in attitude if not in age.

It's all about choice. Deirdre Purcell, the novelist and broadcaster, has written that around the age of sixty she came to the realisation that she would never again fit into a size ten dress and that nobody, including herself, cared. A healthy confident approach to ageing, that. Interestingly, though, when she writes her script for *It Says in the Papers* on RTÉ Radio 1, Deirdre is scrupulously current in her language. She has to be – and that's where the choice comes in. If someone retires in their sixties, they can use whatever language they like; otherwise, they may need to update the way they communicate.

Retired or unretired, it's worth avoiding some of the deadly sins of ageing communication.

1. *'I always say…'*
At any age, this is the trademark of the bore. Where's the virtue in quoting yourself? You're not Mark Twain or Stephen Fry. And, let's face it, if whatever you're always saying was effective any of the previous times you said it, why would you have to repeat it?

2. *'I have to say…'*
Another old bore trademark. You have to say? No, you don't. The odd thing about this phrase is that it's invariably used to introduce an opinion for which the speaker hasn't been asked.

If they want you to say something, they'll ask you. If they haven't, silence is a great option.

3. *'There's nothing in the paper, these days.'*
The minute you find yourself wanting to say this, think of it as a little red light going on in your head, warning you

about mental withdrawal from current events. The more you engage, the more you learn, whether it's the name of the shopping mall in Nigeria where the massacre happened or the name of the president of Egypt, the more positive your ageing will be.

4. *Confirming with pride that your grandchild programmes the device recording TV programmes for later viewing*
Ask your grandchild to teach you and sign off on your new skill. Then both of you will have something to be proud of.

Saturated fat: What was going to kill us all, five years ago. Now it's going to save us all and even make us thin if we put it in coffee.

Scenic route: The road more travelled by those with a genetic inability to get to the shagging point.

Scoop: What nobody in mainstream media gets any more, because the internet has turned potential scoops into runcible spoons.

Screamer: Sub-editor slang for an exclamation mark. The rule used to be: 'If what you've said is funny or outrageous, the reader will get it. You don't need to add a screamer to it.' However, the screamer has made a triumphalist return in texts, where it comes not in single file but in battalions, indiscriminately mustered after sentences of no particular importance.

Screenshot: Taking pictures of a photo, message or internet site from the iPhone or iPad for a purpose, not always positive. For example, if A sends a communication to B using Whatsapp, it will disappear within seconds. Which, in theory, means that if A regrets sending it to B, A is cushy, because it's all gone, bye-bye.

Unless B has taken a screenshot of it, in which case they can send the resultant picture to half a million of their followers ensuring that it will live forever and ever in cyberspace, making a fool of A for all time or at least until climate change drowns us all.

Scroth: The mineral sediment left in the bottom of the glass after consumption of soluble painkillers or other medicine. Good dregs, in other words. Except when the term is applied to someone else. Describing someone as a scroth is not a compliment.

Sea cucumber: The sea cucumber is the canary in the mine of ocean diversity. A luxury food in Asia, its numbers have fallen by 98 per cent. Whereas the scombridge family of fish, including mackerel and tuna, has fallen in number only by 74 per cent in the last thirty years.

Seagull: An airborne predator lacking socials skills which got its fifteen minutes of fame in the summer of 2015.

Search-engine optimisation: The weird paradox of search-engine optimisation is when you Google the companies that do it, why don't they all come up Number 1?

Secret: The Mafia line was that two people could keep a secret if one of them was dead. Increasingly, when people develop serious illnesses like cancer, they publish blogs, columns, diaries or books about their experience, many of them also making TV programmes. Which is why the death of Joan Collins, author of more than thirty 'bonkbuster' bestsellers, caused such a stir, happening six days after her last public appearance and six days after she had given her last interview – to *People* magazine – in which she announced that she was suffering from terminal breast cancer. What startled people was that she had known about her illness for more than half a decade, yet had kept it a secret from everybody other than her own children. This had allowed her to publish several books and undertake international author tours, which, according to research conducted by

BUPA, is why a fifth of men and a quarter of women diagnosed with cancer keep it to themselves: they want to get on with normal life for as long as they can. 'We are finding more patients choosing to keep their diagnosis to themselves and dealing with treatment on their own, or until they've come to terms with it,' a BUPA spokeswoman said.

Self-esteem: A curious, difficult-to-measure factor causative of everything from spree-killing to getting fat.

Oddly, it has been suggested that in New York, the group with the highest self-esteem is made up of teenage African-American boys, while the group with the lowest is made up of white teenage girls.

Large numbers of the first group end up dead by their mid-twenties, while the majority of the second group will be more successful in life than the first group. Go figure.

Self-hatred: Liane Moriarty: 'It drove her to distraction the way women wanted to bond over self-hatred.'[*]

Self-limiting: Description of 90 per cent of illnesses. Cannot be applied to Ebola, rabies or a broken pelvis but means that you probably don't need the antibiotic you're nagging the GP for.

Self-published: Once the last refuge of the failed novelist, now legit. Roddy Doyle was the first outstanding Irish example of the practice. He has been joined by people like Rachel Abbott, who started to write when she retired, decided she might as well self-publish and ended up, in 2015, as the most popular self-published writer in Britain, selling more than a million of her psychological thrillers to Kindle readers.

---

[*]   Liane Moriarty, *Big Little Lies*, New York: Penguin, 2014.

Her four books are priced at about four Euro apiece, out of which she nets 70 per cent. Understandably, she says she has no plans to sign up with a mainstream publisher. Or get herself an agent. Or a publicist. Six self-published authors figure in Kindle's top hundred bestselling writers, based on British sales.

Self-referential: Trend in radio advertising that started in 2008. Every second radio commercial was about advertising copy-writers trying to come up with the killer description of their client's product, or about voice-over artists making a cobblers of reading those killer descriptions, corrected by a disembodied voice ostensibly from the control room. A sweet reminder that, going back to Dorothy L. Sayers and *Mad Men*, everybody in advertising thinks they are the coolest, funniest, sexiest people alive.

Selfie: Self-taken photograph used to share one's new clothes/ weight loss/boyfriend/encounter with a celeb. Self-soothing ritual of the decade.

Selfie stick: Device to allow more people to be crammed into a selfie. Forbidden in many public places, including the Vatican.

Sell-by date: Sell-by dates are for sissies. If you can breathe in when you share a room with it, if it isn't wearing a green fur coat and if it's not capable of walking by itself, eat it.

Semi-casual: Dress code of start-ups and established companies desperately trying to maintain relevance. Makes dressing an expen-sive annoyance. Particularly dastardly when used in the articulated dress code for job interviews: Russian roulette in wardrobe terms.

Sense of humour: What everybody thinks they have, especially those who don't.

Sensitive: Self-exculpatory self-description favoured by the paranoid, the touchy and the hypochondriac.

It is said that when Cosimo de Medici was getting old, he got sensitive. This happens when you're rich, paranoid and afflicted by rheumatism and gout, all of which he was. His wife became irritated by his habit of screaming as if in agony when he was carried in his chair towards a doorway.

'Why do you scream so?' she asked. 'Nothing has happened.'

'If anything had happened,' came the response, 'it wouldn't be any use screaming.'

Serifs: The horizontal lines at the top and bottom of letters in a font like Times New Roman, as opposed to the repellent Arsenal, which is a sans serif font. In other words, it has no serifs. Sans serif fonts are common on computer screens because serifs can jiggle on-screen. However, because serifs are a set of rails, helping the reader's eye roll smoothly over print, tracking the direction of thought, a serif face should always be used in hard copies of speeches and scripts.

Share: Always applied, with misplaced enthusiasm, to the un-stopped venting of pointless personal viewpoints. Nobody ever arrives into your office offering to share last week's Lotto winnings.

Shareholder value: The essential duty of board members in public companies, which can lead to egregious secret-keeping. In 2015 General Motors in the US was ordered to pay roughly a third of a year's income to the families of victims of a deadly fault in their cars, about which they had known even before the cars went on sale. A faulty ignition switch incorporated in GM cars caused the deaths of a hundred and twenty people. GM knew the switch didn't work reliably before they sold the car. They knew it didn't work reliably when reports and complaints came in. They knew it didn't work when drivers began to die – they had to have known, because they settled with the lawyers representing the dead drivers. But they shrouded the whole issue in secrecy and continued to sell their killer product. The dead drivers were expendable. Just as – a century earlier – sufferers from mesothelioma were expendable, as far as the asbestos industry was concerned. Just as smokers were expendable, as far as Big Tobacco was concerned. Just as the whole lot of us were expendable, as far as Exxon was concerned, when it concealed research it had commissioned proving, as long ago as the 1970s, that climate change was a major threat. The directors of each of these corporations could shrug and say that their first duty was to protect shareholder value. It's more than time international governments changed that and put a duty of care to workers and citizens above the duty of care to shareholders.

Sharing economy: Original term for not-for-profit movement to use the internet to improve communities. Now dominated by multi-million-dollar companies using the term to avoid government regulations, health and safety guidelines and a range of taxes. Like Uber.

Should've gone to Specsavers: Great advertising slogan adopted by the public to comment on mistakes. Half a century ago, a Toyota car advertisement achieved much the same currency. The car was the Solara and the slogan was 'Saw your Solara at…' with the vehicle being spotted in all sorts of prestigious locations designed to stroke the self-esteem of the potential owner. Unfortunately, at a certain point, Irish wit took over, with phrases like 'Saw your Solara at the pawnbroker/brothel.' The ad campaign didn't continue for long thereafter.

Shout out: Phrase beloved of radio presenters who spin the wheels of steel and 'Give a shout out to Mary Devaney who's celebrating her golden wedding anniversary today. Card sent in by her eight children, twenty-two grandchildren and thirty-seven great-grand-children.'

'Give a shout out' has largely replaced 'Give a mensh', which was short for 'mention.' We can't make up our minds if we're glad or sorry.

Sick: One of the down-with-the-kids sense reversals with a limited shelf life, like 'bad' being deployed to signify 'good'. Used to describe something that is much admired, for example, 'She has a sick new kitchen,' or, 'That dress is totally sick.'

Single issue candidate: Personification of the bile, misery and failed dreams of mainly rural voters. The local issue that might get one of these candidates elected is always inversely important, relative to what matters to their area and the country, long-term. Becoming less important, when it comes to securing hospital services, new roads or other locally-important infrastructure. However, depending on the result of the next general election, this could change.

Singleton: Bachelor and spinster have fallen into disrepute as descriptors for unhitched individuals. Bachelor because of a growing realisation that it was a cover term for gay men in the closet. Spinster because it came to be seen as pejorative, which it wasn't, referring back, as it did, to a singular craft skill.

Singleton is emerging as the preferred term for those who don't like arguments, hate being upset by conflict and who see marriage or partnership as fraught with both. A study of more than four thousand New Zealanders ranging in age from the late teens to the nineties found that many of the single people were extremely happy to be on their own, despite earlier research suggesting that loners tended to be less happy and healthy than couples.

Singing off the same hymn sheet: Odd usage which came into fashion to describe agreement precisely when most people had forgotten, if they ever knew, what a hymn sheet was.

Sit back and relax: Instruction given by pilots to the souls making up their payload, each of whom is in a seat rendering the instruction null and void.

Skills and drills: Shorthand for repetition and checklisting, both vital to any complex task.

Skip diver: One who shamelessly climbs into other people's skips to retrieve furniture, wood for the stove and bockety chairs. Writer Rita Mae Brown put herself through university in the US by skip-scavenging antiques and flogging them. Recessions take skips off the street but fortunately they're making a comeback, thereby offering opportunities to skip divers.

Slab: A six-pack on steroids.

Sledging: Method of communication used by practitioners of sport to disprove the old saw that it's not the winning or the losing that matters but just the taking part. Uh, uh. The way sledgers see it, distracting other players to ensure they play badly is as good a way of winning as, well, winning.

So they sneak up on another football player just before a crucial section of the match and show him his pregnant girlfriend's telephone number tattooed down their arm while asking the question: 'How d'you think I got that, then?' Or imply they've had sex with the player's mother. Or say something about a recent family tragedy so vile that the player being tortured cannot fail to react.

It's safe to predict that within a few years, athletes will be forced to wear body cameras and voice recorders – like American police officers – to force them to be sportsmanlike.

Slew: Bunch of. Used more by Americans than by Irish people. Which is odd, since it comes from the Irish word *slua*, like Kybosh (see page 108).

Slow-melting ice cream: Never mind the better mousetrap, this is what we all needed: an ingredient that, in the summer heat, would prevent an ice cream cone from melting all over its owner's hands and clothes. Scientists in Edinburgh and Dundee universities have discovered a protein that will slow the melt, so this phrase is on its way to becoming common currency.

Smart phone tyranny: The tyrants, having outsourced their brain and particularly their memory to their phone, live in moment-by-moment terror of failure to record what's going on around them.

The actor Benedict Cumberbatch, playing Hamlet, was so distracted by smart phone wielders filming him in mid-performance that he had to go back to the beginning of 'To be or not to be...' and start over.

The irony was that, after the curtain came down, when he remonstrated outside the theatre with the smart phone tyrants, most of them filmed him while he reproached them.

Smile: The free gift within everybody's power. Should be given without strings attached. Not like Raymond Chandler's description: 'She gave me a smile I could feel in my hip pocket.'

Smoking ban: Genius and risky move made by Mícheál Martin, when he was Minister for Health. Like the passing of the Marriage Equality Referendum much later, this put Ireland on the front page of newspapers all over the world and has made a tangible improvement to Ireland's health.

And not just to Ireland's health: stillbirths in Britain, according to an Edinburgh University team, have dropped by almost 8 per cent since the ban came in there.

Snooze button: An evil device on your clock or phone or both designed to simultaneously appeal to and punish the weak part of your character. Hitting this button gets you the least productive kind of sleep, so you end up going to work ashamed of yourself, possibly late and sleep-hungover.

So: A conversational filler more irritating than 'eh'. It appears in answer to a simple question.

Example: 'Do you like coffee?'

'So. If I had a choice, I would prefer tea.'

Socialise: Used to mean having a good time with pals. (That's now known as binge drinking.) To socialise now means to run an idea or a document past people who might be interested, like quote sluts and stakeholders.

Social media: Electronic toilet door where you pay to be abused and have your life threatened by total strangers.

Solution: An all-purpose business word meaning nothing in particular which offers solace to the lazy and linguistically challenged.

Speak truth to power: A phrase used by advisers to politicians who are not winning, categorising losing as particularly noble and due only to the stupid intransigence of the politician, never to the poor communication of the adviser or the political impracticality of what is proposed.

Sped: Lovely American past tense meaning 'got the hell out of there at speed'. Should be adopted this side of the Atlantic.

Spend more time with my family: Rationale advanced for their resignation by those caught doing bad stuff in the workplace.

Spin doctor: A much misused term from which present company has suffered. It started logically, with guys like sailors. In the days when sailing meant being stuck on a ship for a long time (assuming the ship did not encounter a lethal storm) with a bunch of other guys, sans internet, sans television, sans radio, a sailor who was a willing and able storyteller was Mr Popularity.

Indeed, some novelists, like Jack London, learned some of their skills on board ship. One way or the other, sailors have always had a reputation for spinning yarns and it has been assumed that any yarn spun by a sailor would be akin to a yarn spun by a fisherman – might have fiction heavily threaded through it. In 1812 came what may be the first printed reference in James Hardy Vaux's survey of what he called 'flash language': 'Yarning or spinning a yarn, signifying to relate their various adventures, exploits and escapes to each other.'

Inevitably, in the 20th century, the notion of spinning a semi-fictional yarn began to surface in relation to professionals other than sailors. In 1978, for example, a *Guardian* reporter observed that '…the CIA can be an excellent source [of information], though, like every other, its offerings must be weighed for factuality and spin.'

The term made a leap into politics in the 1980s, when the realisation sank in that television and to a lesser extent radio were going to be of pivotal importance to the careers of individual politicians and that, as a result, media trainers and PR executives would be needed by those politicians. Some of those media trainers and PR executives knew their place, particularly media trainers, for the very good reason that a good media trainer ensures that their political clients can coherently answer for themselves. However, in the US, not all of them saw that line of distinction quite so clearly as those in Ireland. American communications consultants affiliated to a particular client emerged from the shadows and after a public or media appearance by their client, would themselves move in front of the cameras.

It quickly became a regular event, as *The New York Times*, in October 1984, described the aftermath of such a TV outing by a politician: 'A dozen men in good suits and women in silk dresses will circulate smoothly among the reporters, spouting confident opinions. They won't be just press agents trying to impart a favour-able spin to a routine release. They'll be the spin doctors, senior advisers to the candidates.'

By the time Bill Clinton ran for office, his man James Carville, him of the too-often quoted sign 'It's the economy, stupid', appear-ed with combative frequency on TV during the campaign. He was often counter-spun by his Republican opposite number, Mary Matalin. The pair eventually married, despite professional and political differences. Love conquers all.

The provision of quotes by candidate spin doctors had reached such a level of acceptance by the time the 2016 US presidential campaign began that, at the location of each debate, stands would be set up to house the spin doctors affiliated to a particular candidate.

TV crews knew that they would get further comment from every candidate's mouthpiece, with the exception of Donald Trump, who eschewed a spin doctor's services, presumably on the basis that he was capable of mouthing off on his own and, secondarily, much preferred the sound of his own voice to that of a hired hand.

Ireland has no tradition of people from media training, PR or an advertising agency hired by a candidate or party putting out members of its staff to justify or defend the candidate. The nearest we come to it is when former advisers (Gerard Howlin or Fergus Finlay, for example) appear on mainstream media to comment on the successors of the men they advised.

Spiral: The only cool way to serve what nobody wants to eat anyway, like courgettes and cucumbers.

Spire: The definitive waste of money and space, set down in the middle of Dublin city to say something about Ireland that none of us has ever understood. It is tall and skinny, has a light on top, is difficult to clean and repels all attempts by citizens to engage with it in any way. Replaced Nelson's Pillar, which, before it was blown up in the middle of the night by the IRA, was, our grannies tell us, quite a fun experience to climb, largely because it existed in the days before panic attacks. You committed to climbing the spiral stairs up to the admiral, you kept going.

Spoiler alert: Journalistic ass-covering to protect commentators from the ridiculous rage of those who don't want to know about a plot twist until it twists right in front of them.

Stage fright: The normal and proper nervousness felt by performers before trying to entertain an audience. Usually disappears after the first few minutes of the performance. The definitive exception was what happened Barbra Streisand during a live concert in New York in the 1960s:

'I forgot the words [to the song] in front of 125,000 people and I wasn't cute about it or anything,' she remembers. 'I was shocked. I was terrified.'

Streisand didn't undertake another live performance for a quarter of a century.

Stakeholder: Anyone interested in an issue. Used to make the process of letting people know what they should know sound more important and complicated than it is. Also used to make public relations executives sound more important than they are.

Stalking: A relatively modern crime. Up to the 20th century, people were too busy surviving to go stalking others. Now greatly facilitated by technology. One of the most serious threats to the sanity of others, wrongly interpreted – particularly by the stalker – as an indication of undying love.

The majority of staking cases in Ireland are former partners or jilted lovers who won't take no for an answer. They are often emotionally abusive control freaks who dominated their partner in the relationship and viewed them as a possession. The big mistake is to try to let them down gently. They should be taken seriously.

All your friends should be warned against giving them your email address, real address or telephone number. If one of them gives the number, change your phone, conceal the number when you ring even your closest friends and share the number only with people as dedicated to protecting you as you are. Get off Facebook.

Standout: Exceptional or unique.

Star baker: Trademark phrase that got the Duchess of Cambridge's mother into trouble in 2015, when she advertised items on her Party Pieces website with the sentence 'Star Baker essentials are here'. *The Great British Bake-Off* people moved on her like the marines, with suggestions that she was misleading her customers by making it look as if she was connected to the show. (We would have thought she had rather more important connections but we are, apparently, wrong about this.)

'The protection of our intellectual property is something we take seriously,' a spokesman for the production company said, establishing that 'intellectual property' can be applied to pots and pans. Maybe even to paper cupcake containers.

Statesman: Description of a politician who has aged into pomposity. The minute a male politician gets grey hair, some spin doctor will decide he needs to be 'more statesmanlike'.

No female equivalent exists. That's because female politicians, once they hit a certain age, have to concentrate on surviving, rather than posing. Which is just as well. As Harry Truman said, 'A statesman is a dead politician.'

Strange: How liberals describe anything that doesn't fit their mindset. 'X made a very strange point.' No, he didn't. He made a perfectly sensible comment you just didn't like.

Strategy: Long-term, broad-spectrum vision of what is to be done. Constantly misused in order to make plans and methods look more important than they are.

Stress: What stops us becoming under-achieving slugs. We have less to worry about than generations fifty or a hundred years ago but we worry just as much, if not more.

Our resilience levels have dropped and we pay for lessons in mindfulness, which is commonsense with a new name. As in: 'Don't catastrophise about what could happen a week from now. Concentrate on what you're doing at the moment.'

Alternatively, fish are emerging as stress-killers. Watching tropical fish in an aquarium has been scientifically proven by the UK's National Marine Aquarium and the University of Exeter to boost mood while lowering blood pressure and heart rate: 'In times of higher work stress and crowded living, perhaps aquariums can step in and provide an oasis of calm and relaxation,' suggests Dr Sabine Pahl, an associate professor of psychology.

Which does rather ignore the stresses of cleaning out the aquaria and worrying about power cuts.

Study: Method used by health scientists to reputationally self-aggrandise while confusing the hell out of the public.

Thousands of people in this country will read about health today with an enthusiasm they don't bring to any other aspect of the news. They will fall with particular relish on any new study suggesting a particular food can: a) make you thin; b) make you happy, or; c) prevent dementia. Because they're the three triggers. Everybody wants to be thin, happy and sound in the head for as long as possible and as a result, people amend their behaviour in the light of the best incoming information. So, when the best incoming information said that the fats in butter would give you heart disease, harden your arteries and damage you in all sorts of other ways, good conscientious health groupies opened their fridge, looked at the gold-wrapped block of butter and said, 'You're the enemy.' Margarine was adopted as the rescue remedy and the sales of butter took a nose dive.

Of course we missed it. We really did miss it. That dab of butter slithering into the embrace of a bowl of hot petit pois or losing its grip on a corn-on-the-cob. That spoonful inviting a fork on the baked spud or a spoon on the hard-boiled egg.

Oh yes, we missed butter a lot but we were taking care of ourselves the way our mother always said we should, based on scientific evidence, and we had nothing but contempt for people we saw lashing butter on to their food. They would die young, so they would and they would deserve it. Definitely.

The smack in the face to that particular brand of smugness came in the form of another study – a recent one, bigger and better than previous ones – saying: 'No, lads, got it wrong: butter is your only man and those other spreads aren't half as good for you as once was thought.'

Well, thanks a bunch, some of us thought. All that deprivation for damn all benefit? Or, worse still, all that deprivation to achieve a poorer outcome than if butter had been consumed all the way along?

This one followed the news that multivitamin tablets were no good for you and that bread could ruin your life.

Having been brought up on the belief that multivitamin capsules would substitute for anything missing in a less-than-perfect diet, we have now been told that people who have taken them regularly all their lives have nothing to show for it and might have been better off saving their cash and spending it on butter.

The bread issue is part of that theory about prehistoric folk who, we're told, never ate grain and were so much healthier as a result. Never mind that there's no evidence to prove they never ate grain. Or that most of them lived even into their thirties. Paleo diets have swept the world in recent times and anybody seen scoffing a baguette (with butter, of course) has been viewed as gratuitously self-destructive.

On top of all that comes the study taking the ground from under fish oils as a method of preserving the brain power of the people who take them. Not so long ago, the scientists indicated that fish oil would allow people to do master's degrees in their nineties.

Well, maybe they didn't go that far but they certainly promulgated the notion that fish oil+brain=great end results. In the recent past, this has been changed, by the latest study, to fish oil+brain=nothing in particular.

Dubliners of an earlier generation had a great phrase they used in changeable weather: 'You wouldn't know what to pawn.' It's a bit like that in the face of a tsunami of confusing health studies – you wouldn't know what to eat, drink or rub on yourself. The most annoying thing about it is that it proves our mothers right. Moderation in all things seems to be what works. Still.

Subject matter expert: Expert. Banking expert. Tax expert. Ballet expert. The 'subject matter' manages to be simultaneously redundant and imprecise.

Sudoku: A puzzle, refined by the Japanese, where a player inks numbers one to nine into a grid made up of nine squares subdivided into a further nine smaller squares so every number appears once in each horizontal line, vertical line and square. The question is why.

Suffice to say: Not just a cliché. A cliché wrongly stated. It's 'Suffice it to say.' Not that it matters. This one should have received its P45 aeons ago.

Sugar craft: Something Twink does to cakes wearing a white coat. (Twink wearing the white coat, not the cakes, which, as far as we can tell, are naked when she starts with them.)

Suicide: A choice that leaves those around the dead person devastated by their own lack of understanding, due to failure to understand the definition by A.A. Alvarez: 'Suicide is a closed world with its own irresistible logic.'

Supermodel: Used by the girls (see page 88) to describe a photo of herself posted by one of them. The word 'stunning' is also used.

Supportive: Term used by the girls (see page 88) to cover occasional uninterrupted listening to one of their number moaning about her spouse/partner/boss/teenager.

Surreal: Unreal. Frequently used by witnesses to an accident or those who have a mildly unusual experience. When you are surprised by what's happening, it may seem unreal.

Unless what's happening is that a goldfish is tap dancing across your bedroom windowsill dragging a melted pocket watch behind it, surreal it isn't.

Synergy: Adding one and one together, getting three and being delighted with the outcome.

T

T-bone: Vivid borrowed Americanism to describe a vehicular collision in which one car drives straight into the side of another, usually at a crossroads. Or it can be a car driving into a cyclist, although, given the number of cyclists who break red lights and ignore red stop signs, it's a miracle the term is not more popular.

Tablet: Device beloved of people who believe themselves to be busy because they're liking stuff on Facebook.

Takeaway: No longer applied to fish and chips and pizza. Applied, instead, to a thought or fact or implication a speaker at a conference, seminar or company meeting wants people to remember – and 'take away'.

Takeout: A domestic cop out.

Target: Is a noun. Meaning that roundy thing fat guys throw darts at in English pubs. Morons use it as a verb when what they mean is 'aim at'. This is a lost cause but sad, nonetheless.

TATT: Tired all the time. The acronym of the put-upon.

Tattoo: A permanent form of self-expression which used to be the prerogative of sailors. Now, everybody has one, including several celebs who have tattoos recording their never-ending love for another celeb, only to discover a few months thereafter that the tattoo had lasted longer than the love affair. We know one tattoo artist who has a client who gets a tattoo whenever he is drunk and then spends several weeks with her while she tattoos over it in order to 'erase' it. Whenever she spots him lowering liquor in a bar, she is tempted to go over and warn him that it might be costly but tends to let him at it.

Talk down the clock: What witnesses at events like the Oireachtas Banking Enquiry think is smart: talk endlessly about nothing in the hope that the questioners won't get to anything. The Oireachtas Banking Enquiry may have set a precedent in that regard: it worked, there.

Taylor Swift: To hyper document your amazing life on social media. So you might post that you're going to 'Taylor Swift the shit out of my trip to Ibiza'. Tends to be accompanied by a photo of you with your besties simultaneously jumping for joy in vintage swim costumes (as swimsuits used to be known).

Teambuilding: An excuse for indulging in irrelevant collective activities like climbing rocks, real or invented, or shooting red paint at colleagues in a wood. During the recession, this stuff died out a bit but it shows signs of being as indestructible as a cockroach, now that managers who cannot inspire, motivate or manage their team have the money to spend on avoidance behaviour.

Tears: The unacknowledged goal of almost all radio/TV interviews with unknowns. When a presenter says 'Our hearts go out to you,' what is meant is: 'Please cry for me, right now.'

Television: A medium that should never have been invented, about which the best comment was made by Katharine Hepburn: 'The wonderful thing about television is that it allows you to rot in public.'

Tell: Word beloved of amateur body language experts, meaning an involuntary gesture on the part of the person observed which yields enormous meaning to the observer. Popular tells include running the forefinger around the inside of the collar, usually interpreted as signifying duplicity and guilt, folding the arms, usually interpreted as indicative of a closed mind, and touching the face, usually interpreted in any one of a multiplicity of negative ways. All these interpretations are complete garbage, nonetheless applied with misplaced confidence, especially to political leaders subjected to a leaders' debate running up to a general election.

Running the forefinger around the inside of the collar can be an attempt to get comfy with a new shirt, bought for the occasion and starch-stiff out of the package. Folding the arms usually means the arm-folder is cold. Touching the face can mean anything from (hand cupping chin) the face-toucher thinking about something to being discomfited by make-up because they don't usually wear it. Most untypical gestures in a stressful situation (like a televised debate) are symptoms of the strange situation, rather than clues to criminality.

Telling it like it is: The crude forthrightness in reckless and graceless politicians beloved of media hacks because it delivers good headlines. Also has a massive appeal to the bored, the chronically discontented and the straight-up gobshite. Best exemplar of telling it like it is, outside this country, is Donald Trump, whose honesty includes calling Mexicans rapists, allowing others to call Barack Obama a Muslim, asking rhetorically who could vote for a face like Carly Fiorina's and bitching about a Fox News broadcaster who asked him a tough question by making reference to her menstruating. What's that you ask? Oh, who is the best exemplar of telling it like it is, inside Ireland? You kidding? Libel laws prevent. Unfortunately.

Terms of endearment: To be used with caution. 'Sweetie', 'Love' and 'Darling' can be received as put-downs and impertinences by women and by older people, although a care home in Britain, ticked off for promiscuous use of such terms by the regulator, said that it was going to continue. 'I understand that they're inspecting lots of places and they may come up against places where condescending language is used in a condescending manner,' the CEO of the home, which cares for people with learning disabilities, said. 'That's not the case in our situation.' All right, honey.

Terrier complex: Lack of realism in some executives, which leads them to believe that no fight is too big for them.

Thanks in advance: Thanking someone for something you may not receive but doing it anyway to manipulate them into sending whatever it is to you.

The proof is in the pudding: Bad enough to use a cliché but to use a cliché wrong is a crime. The cliché is that 'The proof of the pudding is in the eating.' Meaning (just in case you've been living under a pudding-free rock) that until you eat the bloody thing you can't know if you've cooked it correctly. Got that? Good. Then you are unlikely to join the growing group of morons who talk of the proof being in the pudding, as if it made any sense.

Thick: State of extreme emotional retardation experienced by Irish men when angry and/or drunk. Drives men to acts of vigilantism, revenge, stupidity and localised carnage. Unofficially a reasonable defence in court when legal consequences loom.

Third partying: The habit, favoured by politicians but not exclusive to them, of referring to themselves in the third party. 'Joe Bloggs is an honest man,' Joe Bloggs will say, as if referring to himself as an acquaintance deepened the veracity of the claim over simply saying, 'I'm an honest man.'

One of the few politicians who seemed to be aware of third partying their references to themselves was Charles de Gaulle, who observed that because people had a mental personification of de Gaulle: 'I knew that I should have to take account of that man...I became almost his prisoner. Before every speech or decision I questioned myself: is this the way in which the people expect de Gaulle to act? There are many things I should like to have done but that I did not do because they would not have been what they expected of General de Gaulle.'

Thong: A painful and irritating string simulacrum of underpants adored by fans of steatopygia (see page 30), which a thong maximises. The undergarment used by Monica Lewinsky when she flashed at then US president Bill Clinton to provoke him into giving her a book of poetry.

Thongs are falling out of fashion, with Marks & Spencer, the retail knicker capital of the world, showing only one of them in its autumn 2015 collection, as opposed to fourteen real Bridget Jones jobs. In contrast, men are going for tightier whities. (See below.)

Tiffany effect: A bit of unspecial mass-produced jewellery in a Tiffany box will be assumed to be of more value than something hand-made in an unbranded box.

Tighty whities: Men's underwear. Which haven't been that tight in recent years, when boxer shorts made Y-fronts a sweet memory, rather than a current proposition. British underwear retailer the Original Factory Shop, says, however, that Y-fronts are surging back to the front. Their sales of the tighter, snugger underwear more than doubled in 2015.

To be honest with you: Unfortunate phrase, introduced into a conversation or interview to lend added value to what it introduces while in fact it diminishes the value of what preceded it: now we all know it was false since honesty comes into play only with the use of the phrase.

Toilet flushing: Having it off with someone other than your wife, husband, spouse or partner without their knowledge is bad enough. It's still cheating on fidelity even if they do know but let's not get philosophical about it. However, actress Uma Thurman maintains that 'it's better to have a relationship with someone who cheats than someone who doesn't flush the toilet'.

Totes: No, not a shape of handbag but a way of emphasising something. For example, if a movie makes a viewer cry, they may describe it as 'totes emosh'.

Transgender: Being born in the wrongly gendered body. Getting over transitioning to another sex takes effort and time, although most younger people doing it these days report that their peers are supportive. Which makes somewhat odd the amount of coverage about Caitlyn Jenner that credits her with great courage. No. Not really.

It took enormous courage for James Morris to change gender in 1972. Morris was a historian who had produced a definitive work about the British Empire. He had accompanied Sir Edmund Hillary's climb of Everest. He was in his mid-forties, married with children, when he made the same decision Jenner more recently made: that he could not live the rest of his life as a man.

As Jan Morris, she broke down all of the barriers, created all the precedents and re-established herself – in today's terms – as a respected and celebrated brand. Nobody at Jan Morris's level of fame had ever made the gender transition in a public way. She wrote about it.* She talked about it. By so doing and by sustaining the inevitable bigotry thereby occasioned, she created a new possibility in the minds of a generation who had never envisaged the possibility of sex change, no matter how grievously mismatched they felt with their assigned gender.

Admittedly, Jan Morris made her transition prior to the invention of the internet, never mind social media. Which gave her advantages and disadvantages. The market for her books was a reasonably elite, educated, literate and reflective one, likely to continue to accept her offerings because of their intrinsic value. It was also dominated by readers living on this side of the Atlantic. Caitlyn Jenner's market is dominated by viewers and social media consumers living in the US but taking in the rest of the world. Jenner's audience is unreflective and neophiliac. For them, her athletic past belongs in pre-history. Her saleability derives from whatever she does that differs from what she did yesterday.

Caitlyn Jenner will make millions from wearing a bustier and sharing her feelings about her most recent (formerly Kardashian) wife. Jan Morris will continue to earn a modest living from elegantly erudite books about topics indicative of sustained intellectual curiosity. In 2008, sixty years after James Morris and Elizabeth Tuckniss became man and wife, they married again as Jan and Elizabeth Morris, having quietly lived as a couple for the intervening years. It was Morris who changed the world for trans people. Including Caitlyn Jenner.

Transphobic: The prejudice which, until recently, you didn't know you could harbour. Former rapper-turned-standup Mos Def, doing a gig in London, at which he commented about the transition of Caitlyn Jenner, used lines including: 'Some people get freaked out

---

*   Jan Morris, *Conundrum*, London: Faber & Faber, 1974.

when you knew someone as a dude for all of your life and then suddenly they're not a dude any more…don't be so hard on me that I'm just quite freaked out by that.' Members of the audience walked out at that point, calling the performer transphobic.

Transparency: The single most overused, most meaningless bilge term used in political discourse, usually by people talking vaguely but vehemently about reform of some aspect of the parliamentary process about which no normal human being gives much of a toss. It's up there with 'accountability'. Broadcasters love asking if anybody will be held accountable. By which they mean: 'Will someone go to prison?' To which the answer is, nine times out of ten, no.

Travellers: Members of the travelling community. That's what they call themselves. That's what they should be called. For a while there, decent middle-class people thought it would be good to call them itinerants, which, while better than some of the other abusive terms used, is still not right.

Tribalism: The ultimate condemnation, interestingly applied to the normally popular Fr Brian D'Arcy when he participated in a protest about the way the Quinn family (once mega rich, now not so) were being treated by the Revenue Commissioners and others. D'arcy found himself in the 'us' and 'them' situation portrayed so brutally in the novella and movie *Lord of the Flies*. In the national standoff around the Quinn family, each side saw themselves as the 'in' group and viewed the other side as definitively the 'out' group. To be seen as standing publicly with the family, to brave the ever-present cameras and the furious media comment, was interpreted from the point of view of those involved as us (rural commonsense folk grateful for the jobs Sean Quinn delivered in our area) versus them (professionally angry urban commentators).

Brian D'Arcy explained his presence on the Quinn protest lorry as the action of a man 'born and reared in these parts'. He behaved towards people he has known for more than fifty years 'the same way as I would be with any family in trouble'. He called it neighbourliness but was roundly condemned for tribalism. He survived just fine.

Troll: Unemployed, isolated, unattractive smelly failure who gets their kicks from tweeting nasty comments when someone famous and troubled, like Robin Williams, takes their own life.

Truffle oil: One of those pantry items no ordinary person has. Always found, on the other hand, in the kitchen cupboards of the upwardly mobile.

Trusted adviser: The best and most difficult role in the world and no, we're not talking about 'How do you feel about that?' life-coaching. 'Ambitious professionals invest tremendous energy in improving business skills,' say the writers of *The Trusted Adviser,* one of the best books for consultants and aspirant consultants, 'including sharpening their specific expertise, gaining experience, broadening their knowledge and "networking", all requiring hard work. However, seldom do they give enough thought to creating trust relationships with clients and little guidance is provided by their firms on how to accomplish this. Many professionals do not know how to think about or examine trust relationships.'

Truth: Morally better. Also safer, because you don't have to re-member a lie.

Twitter: A firehose of crowd-sourced data suffering losses of half a billion dollars last year on a turnover of just three times that figure.

Typewriter: The typewriter is more than a historic artefact. It has changed history and may be making a comeback, because the Russian security guys have decided it's time to go back to the future.

If two blokes like Julian Assange and Edward Snowden, with a little whistleblower assistance, can blow a hole the size of a small kingdom in the security systems of one of the largest and most powerful countries, it's clearly time to take a new look at why it's so easy to get information out of the computers where it should be and into media where – as they see it – it shouldn't be.

The Russians are investing about €12,000 in typewriters. Yes, typewriters. They say that any malicious guy with smarts can download enormous amounts of information from a computer on to a flash drive, whereas if one human being types a crucial document using a typewriter, then if somebody wants to steal and leak that data, they have to photocopy it, which is logistically complicated and time-consuming, or sit with the document and input their own version of it, which is both of the above and also, when it comes to publishing the material, raises the inevitable question: 'How can we know that you didn't sit down with your PC on an insomniac night and just make up all this stuff?'

So it's back to the typewriter, the technology that arguably changed more lives than any previously-invented communications machinery.

The typewriter was at least as effective, when it came to liberating women from their roles as powerless chattels of their menfolk, as were the more publicised actions of the suffragettes.

Women's hands seemed suited to keyboards and their brains copped on to the QWERTY layout of those keyboards more easily than did the male brain at the time. So many of them started to work outside the home and establish their own personal revenue streams that one historian suggests that a leap in the numbers of rapes was a direct consequence. Men were deeply threatened by this new female freedom and personal assertion, so the theory goes, and took to raping women as a violent demonstration of their power.

U

Under the bus: Wasn't me, Guvnor, was him.

Unmediated communication: In mediaeval society, people relied on the local clergy as opinion leaders and information deliverers. The Church held the truth and also perfected the courier system. Plus they were storytellers who provided their own visuals in the form of the rose windows in the cathedrals, which provided the pictures for the Biblical stories they told to help their parishioners learn, evaluate, interpret and respond to essential information.*

Every time a new method of communication, such as the printed word, emerged, communication moved further away from being totally owned by an elite.

Up all night to get lucky: The video that sums up the best of 2013, starring PR executive Andrea Pappin and a taxi driver named Wayne Karney. The external speakers belonging to a Dublin pub, on an evening in the first week of July, in the middle of an exceptionally warm dry summer, were broadcasting Daft Punk's song 'Get Lucky' to people drinking pale ale or coffee outside, as the sun slowly set.

---

*   Sophia Menache, *Vox Dei: Communication in the Middle Ages*, Oxford: Oxford University Press, 1990.

Location? Off Dame Street, close to Dublin Castle. A taxi meandered up and was brought to a halt by what looked like a one-person street party. The driver watched a young woman bopping to the music in the middle of the street and, so infectious was the music, began, seated in his vehicle with the windows rolled down, to bop along. The young woman spotted this, ran over to him and dragged him out of the taxi to dance with her.

The two of them then danced in the slanted evening sun, as passersby stopped passing by. Instead, they halted. To watch. To nod. To smile. To vicariously participate in a spontaneous celebration of a great song, of an entertaining moment and of the summery atmosphere.

It was dancing at the crossroads, updated, and several bright sparks caught it all on their mobile phones, uploading it so that people who have never been in that particular street could, from several different angles, see what happened. Two individuals who were complete strangers to each other totally enjoyed themselves – lived in the moment, if you'll pardon the Oprah-ism – for just under three minutes.

They amused those who were there on the day and virally entertained thousands more.

Eventually the taxi driver, who is some mover, decided he needed to get back to the day job and – still dancing – returned to his car, accompanied by his dancing partner, who tried a jive move with him before he mimed a joke about the boot of his car. She reacted with pretended outrage and danced away from him while he sat back in the driver's seat. Just as he was about to depart, the girl he'd been dancing with ran back over to the vehicle – still clutching a glass out of which not a drop seemed to have been spilled – and gave him a parting kiss. The crowd applauded and the red taxi reversed away from the scene. End of story. Beginning of shared memory.

It's not an important or significant memory. It makes no major statement about life or society. It just shows Ireland's indestructible gift for spontaneity, our capacity to make fun out of very little and how pretty our capital city is on a sunny summer evening. It may have happened towards the end of a grievous recession but nothing captured by the cameras shows that. What's captured is uncomplicated infectious happiness.

No similar song or event happened in 2014 or 2015.

Upward only rent review: A long way of saying a method of killing off commercial tenants.

V

Validation: Curiously, constantly demanded of others by those most addicted to self-help.

Values: Word mistakenly used by companies when what is meant are 'corporate aspirations'. Values are lived over time. And – for individuals – how you spend your time and your money establishes the essence of your values.

VBF: Abandoned term replaced by 'bestie'. Largely meaningless, as when applied to Joan Baez when she appeared in a picture with Taylor Swift. Joan Baez may be many things but Taylor Swift's bestie she isn't.

Very: An intensifier that weakens and is over-used.

Very unique: Can't be. Unique means one of a kind. It's an absolute. Like dead. You can't be very dead. Nor can you be very unique.

Veteran: Term for anybody who's been doing the same thing for a long time.

Vibrant: How dying political parties always describe themselves.

Victim: The safest thing to be. Once properly validated, the victim is impregnable, untouchable and ineffable. It is, however, something of an over-supplied market and the term is losing its impact as a result.

Victim-blaming: Considerably worse than shooting the messenger, even when the blamer is also the victim, as happened when Chrissie Hynde, lead singer with the Pretenders, blamed herself for being forced to perform sex acts on members of a violent gang when she was twenty-one. Now sixty-three, Hynde told *The Sunday Times* that she took 'full responsibility' for what happened.

'Technically speaking, however you want to look at it, this was all my doing and I take full responsibility,' she said. 'You can't fuck about with people, especially people who wear "I Heart Rape" and "On Your Knees" badges…those motorcycle gangs, that's what they do.'

Now on a roll, the singer suggested that what women wear can 'entice' a rapist and that wearing low heels helped women run away from rapists.

Hynde's comments were condemned by the managers of rape crisis centres.

Vigilance committee: Quaint secretive committee run by the GAA up to the 1970s to spy on members attending banned foreign games. It really existed. Honestly.

Vindicated: Politicians think this word means 'not guilty' or even, at a stretch, 'innocent'. The rest of us think it's the equivalent of the old Scottish verdict 'not proven'. Clean guilty, rather than dirty guilty.

Vision: The thing managers are supposed to have, in companies where it isn't required. Managers respond to this unneeded need by taking other managers to luxury hotels for a day or a weekend, where a highly-paid facilitator gets them to say the obvious and write it down on sheets torn from an oversized display jotter. This bunch of banalities is then crafted into a vision or mission statement to which nobody ever pays a blind bit of attention.

Vitamins and exercise: Cure for depression, according to Dr (not) Tom Cruise.

Vomitorium: Streets of Irish cities on Friday and Saturday nights.

W

Walk: The way you walk is gender specific, as two would-be robbers found out in London in 2015 when they held up a pawnshop while dressed in burkas. Passersby realised they 'didn't walk like women' and alerted the cops. Who arrested and disrobed the two men.

Waiting time: When research has been done on people queuing in a business, the research invariably finds that the customer's estimate of time elapsed since their arrival greatly exceeds the reality. A customer waiting for forty seconds may believe the delay lasted four minutes.

Walking distance: Everywhere is within walking distance if you have the time.

Walkout: The moment of televisual drama developed to a high art by the late Reverend Ian Paisley. The walker-out must reach high doh, explain what has caused them to reach high doh and exit the studio without losing their trousers to a trailing microphone cable.

The walkout is currently in disrepute, courtesy of trade unionist Jack O'Connor, whose exit from *Tonight with Vincent Brown* was too inept even to enjoy on YouTube. Although Vincent enjoyed it at the time.

Water conservation grant: Payment given to all Irish residents. Has no correlation with said resident's intention to conserve a scarce resource.

Wedge: The ugliest form of footwear known to womankind.

Wellness: Just don't go there, OK?

West Wing: The first TV series that swelled its viewing audience up with a sense of its own virtue.

What?: Once a bad-mannered way of asking someone to repeat what they had just said, this is now a multi-purpose general query, sometimes – particularly in the AIG ads – used with comic intent. Most enjoyable use was by RTÉ newsreader Aengus Mac Grianna, who powdered his nose, tidied his hair, arranged his tie and dusted off his suit before someone on the studio floor attracted his attention to alert him to the fact that all this dapperising was being broadcast. 'What?' was his response. Immortalised on YouTube.

Where are you?: The most frequent opening line in telephone calls. The correct answer is: 'At the end of the line, waiting for you to get to the point.'

White collar crime: The term was first used by a man named Edwin H. Sutherland in 1939 in his presidential address to the American Sociological Society. It covers crimes like the covering up of the dangers of asbestos (even though they'd been known since Ancient Rome), collusion between firms to maintain prices and bribery.

White-out: Every office in Ireland used to have copious tiny bottles of Tipp-ex, partly for erasing typewriter errors, partly because the secretaries who used it liked to sniff it, not knowing they were developing respectable drug habits. (First of the two drug habits that left white marks on the nose of the habitués.) The correction fluid idea came from a smart secretary named Bette Nesmith Graham, who earned extra cash by painting Santa and other holiday figures on to the windows at the bank where she worked, in the course of which, she later said, she copped on that 'An artist never corrects by erasing but always paints over the error. So I decided to use what artists use. I put some tempera water-based paint in a bottle and took my watercolor brush to the office. I used that to correct my mistakes.'

Graham refined her mixture with the help of her son's chemistry teacher at Thomas Jefferson High School in Dallas. Her son was named Mike and later became one of the singing group called The Monkees. Bette decided to market what she first called Mistake Out in the mid-1950s, later setting up her own company to sell the renamed Liquid Paper and become a millionaire. Fifty years later, it had been rendered largely obsolete by computers and printers.

Whoa person: Essential family or company member. Just when an idea is about to take off, they deflate it. This can be tedious but does prevent the eventual ownership of three worthless Polish apartments.

Wide boy: The Irish wide boy: always on the margins of honesty, clever, insightful (particularly about what people really think, as opposed to what they righteously should think), witty, charming, celebrated by Boucicault and O'Casey, who always comes in a side door even when the front door is wide open.

Wifi: Pronounced 'Wiffy', according to an educationalist and politician.

Winching: Cool action of the search-and-rescue gals, who bring their helicopter in alongside the cliff you were dumb enough to get stuck on, lower a lad on a string to put you in a harness and have you wound back up into the chopper. Also used, increasingly, to remove the morbidly obese from their homes when knocking down the door and the door frame won't suffice. This, of course, fails to address the fact that the morbidly and bed-bound obese couldn't get that way without the active criminal support of 'friends' and relatives. It's illegal to help someone to a fast, efficient suicide but perfectly legal to help someone to a slow, inefficient, humiliating and costly suicide.

With all due respect: Introduces the rudest, least respectful comment possible.

Work: Up there with love as what makes life worth living. Especially if you enjoy it and the people you work with. 'To love what you do and feel that it matters – how could anything be more fun?' Katharine Graham, who owned the *Washington Post* in the Watergate years.

Work-life balance: A ludicrous notion advanced by the lazy to explain why they never achieve anything.

Working on the chakras: No. Not an 18th-century penal colony in Oceania. The chakras are energy points on the body that spin and need to be opened, rinsed or cleansed. Usually at huge expense and with an outcome so exalted it is seen only by the initiated and at 'the energetic level'. They each have their own colour. With all my chakras fully operational, my third eye is now open. Like the *Skibbereen Eagle*, I have it on you.

Workplace: Where you work. Not where you receive parcels from Amazon. According to banks in Britain like Citigroup, HSBC and JPMorgan, giving your workplace address as the receiving point for your personal deliveries is not acceptable.

They say that almost four out of ten items of incoming mail consist of obviously personal items, an increase, year on year, of 20 per cent. It hasn't yet become something to be banned in Ireland but when it does, it will benefit the receiving units at petrol stations.

Writer's block: A new form of this mythical ailment has been identified by Jonathan Franzen, the award-winning American writer. He says writers today are being paralysed by fears of a social media backlash. 'The fear of being called a bad name [makes it] very hard to be creative, actually. Because you're worried about what you might be called and whether it's fair or not. There used to be rather serious firewalls between the artist and the buying public – the gallery, the publisher. And technology demolishes that wall and basically says: promote or die.'

Y

YOLO: You only live once. We're so over this term.

Your side of the story: Phrase used by journalists who want you to get yourself into even more trouble than you're already in. They're on your side. Of course they are. As long as there's a chance you give legs to their story by offering them quotes. Tip: when your mouth has caused you to enter the world of public disrepute, shut it.

Yuccie: Young urban creatives. Found in cities, these twenty-five to thirty-five year olds work in the creative professions and don't follow trends like hipsters.

Z

Zebra crossing: Road crossing point designated for pedestrians, clearly marked for the benefit of all. Ignored by cyclists.

Zimmer: A device to assist older people who have difficulty walking and sustaining their balance. Although some of these medical aids, first developed in the 1950s, are made by the Zimmer company, many are not. However, 'Zimmer' has become a generic and a pejorative one at that, extrapolated and applied to anyone over sixty years of age.

Bibliography

Bourke, Anthony and John Randall. *A Lion Called Christian.* London: Macmillan, 2009.

Bowe, Valerie. *My Mother Always Used to Say.* Dublin: Londubh Books, 2010.

Callow, Simon. *Orson Welles: Vol. 1 – The Road to Xanadu.* New York: Viking, 1996.

Casey, Ronan. *Medium-Sized Town, Fairly Big Story.* Dublin: Gill & Macmillan, 2014.

Coben, Harlan. *Darkest Fear.* London: Orion, 2002.

Coleman, James William. *The Criminal Elite: The Sociology of White-collar Crime.* New York: St Martin's Press, 1989.

Cytowic, Dr Richard E. *The Man Who Tasted Shapes.* New York: Putnam, 2003.

Gawande, Atul. *The Checklist Manifesto: How to Get Things Right.* New York: Metropolitan, 2009.

Hakim, Catherine. *Erotic Capital: The Power of Attraction in the Boardroom and the Bedroom.* London: Basic Books, 2011.

Harris, Professor David. *The Dental Amputee.* Dublin: Londubh Books, 2015.

Kirwin, Barbara R., PhD. *The Mad, the Bad and the Innocent: Tales of a Forensic Psychologist.* New York: Little, Brown, 1997.

Lahey, Jessica. *The Gift of Failure.* London: Short Books, 2015.

Lindbergh, Reeve. *Beneath a Wing,* Dublin: Poolbeg Press, 2000.

Maister, David H., Charles H. Green and Robert M. Galford. *The Trusted Adviser*. New York: FreePress, 2000.

Mamet, David. *Make-Believe Town: Essays and Remembrance*. New York: Little, Brown, 1996.

Maraniss, David. *The Clinton Enigma*. New York: Simon and Schuster, 1998.

Menache, Sophia. *Vox Dei: Communication in the Middle Ages*. Oxford: Oxford University Press, 1990.

Mischel, Walter. *The Marshmallow Test: Understanding Self-control and How to Master It*. New York: Bantam Press, 2014.

Moriarty, Liane. *Big Little Lies*. New York: Penguin, 2014.

Morris, Jan. *Conundrum*. London: Faber & Faber, 1974.

Peter, Laurence J. and Raymond Hull. *The Peter Principle: Why Things Always Go Wrong*. New York: William Morrow, 1969.

Pogrebin, Letty. *How To Be a Friend to a Friend Who's Sick*. PublicAffairs, 1997.

Sandberg Sheryl. *Lean In: Women, Work, and the Will to Lead*. New York: Knopf, 2013.

Saul, Richard, M.D. *ADHD Does Not Exist: the Truth about ADHD*. New York: Harper Wave, 2014.

Sereny, Gitta. *Albert Speer: His Battle with Truth*. London: Macmillan, 1995.

Spence, Gerry. *O.J. The Last Word*. New York: St Martin's Press, 1997.

Stephanopoulos, George. *All Too Human*. New York: Little, Brown, 1999.

Sulloway, Frank J. *Born to Rebel: Birth Order, Family Dynamics and Creative Lives*. New York: Pantheon, 1996.

Trivers, Robert. *The Folly of Fools: The Logic of Deceit and Self-Deception in Human Life*. New York: Basic Books, 2011.

Vaillant, George E. *Triumphs of Experience: The Men of the Harvard Grant Study*. Harvard: Belknap, 2012.

Vaughan, Peggy. *The Monogamy Myth*. Newmarket Press, 1989.

Wolitzer, Meg. *The Ten Year Nap*. New York, Riverhead, 2008.